ORTHO'S All About

Plans for
Beds & Borders

Meredith® Books
Des Moines, Iowa

Ortho® Books
An imprint of Meredith® Books

Plans for Beds & Borders
Editor: Marilyn Rogers
Writer: Phillip Edinger
Contributing Editors: Doug Jimerson, Studio G
Senior Associate Design Director: Tom Wegner
Assistant Editor: Harijs Priekulis
Copy Chief: Terri Fredrickson
Managers, Book Production: Pam Kvitne,
    Marjorie J. Schenkelberg
Contributing Copy Editors: Barbara Feller-Roth
Contributing Proofreaders: Barbara J. Stokes, JoEllyn Witke
Contributing Illustrators: Lois Lovejoy
Contributing Map Illustrator: Jana Fothergill
Indexer: Ellen Davenport
Electronic Production Coordinator: Paula Forest
Editorial and Design Assistants: Kathleen Stevens,
    Karen Schirm

Additional Editorial Contributions from
    Art Rep Services
Director: Chip Nadeau
Designers: lk Design

Meredith® Books
Editor in Chief: James D. Blume
Design Director: Matt Strelecki
Managing Editor: Gregory H. Kayko
Executive Editor, Gardening and Home Improvement:
    Benjamin W. Allen

Director, Sales, Special Markets: Rita McMullen
Director, Sales, Premiums: Michael A. Peterson
Director, Sales, Retail: Tom Wierzbicki
Director, Book Marketing: Brad Elmitt
Director, Operations: George A. Susral
Director, Production: Douglas M. Johnston

Meredith Publishing Group
President, Publishing Group: Stephen M. Lacy

Meredith Corporation
Chairman and Chief Executive Officer: William T. Kerr
Chairman of the Executive Committee: E.T. Meredith III

Thanks to
Rosemary A. Kautzky, Sandra Neff, Spectrum
    Communication Services, Inc., Mary Irene Swartz

Photographers
    (Photographers credited may retain copyright ©
    to the listed photographs.)
L = Left, R = Right, C = Center, B = Bottom, T = Top
Patricia J. Bruno/Positive Images: 92
Gay Bumgarner/Positive Image: 54, 64, 69T
R. Todd Davis: 18, 80, 81, 82, 107B
Derek Fell: 19, 32, 85R
John Glover/gardenIMAGE: 31
Margaret Hensel/Positive Image: 60
Saxon Holt: 22, 24–25, 29, 100
Pete Krumhardt: 4–5, 10, 12, 14, 15, 20, 21, 27T, 28, 33, 35,
    36, 44, 45, 46, 48, 49, 52, 53, 56, 58R, 63, 67, 69B, 71T,
    72, 74, 75, 85L, 87, 90L, 95R, 99L, 106, 107T
Andrew Lawson/gardenIMAGE: 7, 8
Janet Loughrey: 34, 42, 43, 76–77, 78, 86, 95L, 102, 103
Allan Mandell/gardenIMAGE: 104–105
Ben Phillips/Positive Images: 90R
Richard Shiell: 51, 88–89, 99R
Michael S. Thompson: 37
NanceTrueworthy/gardenIMAGE: 6
Deidra Walpole: 30, 71B

Cover photo by John Glover.

All of us at Ortho® Books are dedicated to providing you
with the information and ideas you need to enhance your
home and garden. We welcome your comments and
suggestions about this book. Write to us at:
    Meredith Corporation
    Ortho Gardening Books
    1716 Locust St.
    Des Moines, IA 50309–3023

If you would like to purchase any of our gardening, home
improvement, cooking, crafts, or home decorating and
design books, check wherever quality books are sold. Or visit
us at: meredithbooks.com

If you would like more information on other Ortho
products, call 800-225-2883 or visit us at: www.ortho.com

Note to the Readers: Due to differing conditions, tools,
and individual skills, Meredith Corporation assumes no
responsibility for any damages, injuries suffered, or losses
incurred as a result of following the information published
in this book.

PLANNING YOUR FLOWER GARDEN 4

SEASONAL GARDENS 10

COLOR GARDENS 24

THEME AND PERIOD GARDENS 38

GARDENS FOR SPECIAL SITUATIONS 76

GARDENS FOR SPECIFIC PLANTS 88

KEEPING YOUR GARDEN IN TOP FORM 104

PLANNING YOUR FLOWER GARDEN

As the pace of life accelerates and time and land assume more value, small things of beauty become increasingly precious. We can savor the grandeur of estate gardens in the sweeping landscapes of parks; but to satisfy our need for personal expression, and to reap the greatest rewards from the least effort, we turn to flower gardening.

Virtually everyone who has the urge to garden imagines being surrounded by beds of colorful flowers. No wonder, then, that a collection of flower garden plans has wide appeal. A flower garden brings the promise of beauty and color on a manageable scale without a great outlay of money or time. Starting one could easily be a weekend do-it-yourself project.

In the following pages are 42 planting plans for gardens that address a variety of needs and interests. Should you need seasonal color, you'll find garden plans specifically for color in each of the four seasons, as well as a plan for a garden that is colorful from spring into fall. Should you want a garden that features a particular color or color group, there are plans for a white garden, a gray garden, gardens devoted to cool, warm, or pastel tones, and ones that get their color from foliage alone.

Another set of plans focuses on particular garden styles; these range from the studied simplicity of Japanese and desert plantings to the exuberance of an English cottage garden. Other plans reflect particular themes, such as the world of nature (hummingbird and butterfly gardens) and literature and history (Shakespeare and medieval apothecary gardens). Gardeners of a practical bent will be interested in the plans for an efficient kitchen garden and for a bed of flowers for cutting. There are plans designed for special situations: a shade planting, a low-water-use planting, and plantings for damp soil, a hillside, and a pond. And gardeners with specific plant interests will find individual plans for annuals, perennials, ornamental grasses, and shrubs, and three different plans for roses—a formal garden, an informal rose garden, and an heirloom rose garden. What's more, all of the garden plans in this book can be easily adapted to any size or shape. Even if you have limited garden space, you can easily shrink these garden plans to a smaller scale.

Hot summer colors of orange hardy lilies and yellow lanceleaf coreopsis cool down with blues and neutral colors from plants such as these feverfew, blue flax, and gray lamb's-ears.

USING THIS BOOK

Spring flower borders tend to bloom in pastel tints. This spring garden includes bearded and Siberian iris, catmint, early daylily, and larkspur.

Each garden is presented in the same way. A planting plan illustrates the arrangement of plants within the garden. Drawn to scale on a grid (one square represents one square foot), it shows the space each plant will occupy. Note that in most cases, the plants are combined in drifts or clumps for best effect.

An artist's rendering illustrates a portion of each plan as it might look in flower.

The photographs give you ideas for varying the plans. Some show similar gardens created from ideas gleaned from this book. Others suggest alternative plants that would work in the design.

The plant list is arranged in this format: A–1–Purple smoke tree (*Cotinus coggygria* 'Royal Purple'). The letters refer to the letters keyed on the planting plan. The number indicates how many of that plant to buy for the garden. The number also represents how many plants should occupy the space allotted. If the plant is in several drifts around the garden, divide the total number listed by the number of clumps.

Next appears the plant's common name followed by its botanical name in parentheses. The name in single quotes is the cultivar name. You may substitute other cultivars with similar size and foliage and bloom colors.

PLANT CHOICE AND CARE

The plants for each plan have been selected to satisfy the widest possible gardening audience. Each plan has at least two lists: a main list and an alternate list. Most main-list plants grow well in Zone 7. (See the United States Department of Agriculture Hardiness Zone Map on page 108.) Most will grow in colder and warmer regions as well. You may also be able to take advantage of the microclimate in your backyard. Beds located in a protected location (along a wall or against a house) may support plants adapted to warmer regions than your normal Zone.

The text for each garden explains the Zone tolerance. The alternative plant lists, which range from a few plants to an entirely different list, have two purposes. In many cases, they extend the usefulness of a plan into much colder or warmer regions. Secondly, where the main plant list is designed to satisfy a broad climate range, the alternative selections list may have plants that will give the garden a different color slant. On some plans you will find alternative selections given for each plant, according to criteria mentioned in the text of the plan.

Aside from Zone tolerance, the other criterion in choosing the plants for these gardens was their availability. No plants are rare, obscure, or hard to locate. Many, in fact, should be carried by well-stocked local nurseries. If you can't find a plant locally, most are also offered by mail-order suppliers and specialty plant nurseries. Most of the annual flowers can be easily grown from seed, if not available locally.

The description of each plan includes some basic information you'll need to ensure success. Although most of the plans have been devised to suit average garden soil and routine watering, you will find the cultural needs spelled out for each planting. And since all gardens need some maintenance to succeed, the text also suggests a suitable program for routine tasks such as pruning, watering, dividing, staking, mulching, weeding, propagation, and deadheading.

VARIATIONS

Each plan was designed as an individual unit, complete unto itself, but you can install any portion of the plantings into an existing garden, provided cultural conditions are suitable. Garden plans can also be mixed and matched. For example, assuming the garden and regional conditions are similar, you could take one section of An Informal Modern-Rose Garden and blend it with a complementary garden plan, such as the Fragrant Garden, the English Cottage Garden, or the Summer Garden.

What do you do if a plan is ideal except that it is too large for your space or is not quite the right configuration? The instructions under Variations will offer at least one way to alter the size or shape of the planting while maintaining an attractive, well-designed flower garden.

Remember, these plans are meant to be only a guide to help you create the garden of your dreams. Half the joy of gardening comes from its unexpected nature, so you need not re-create a particular garden plan down to the smallest detail. Choose a plan that matches your needs, and feel free to change the things you don't like.

As edible as it is ornamental, this colorful border contains pot marigold, nasturtium, and flowering cabbage.

DESIGN BASICS

If you study the plans in this book, you'll quickly discover that they may look dramatically different, but they all have some design basics in common.

FLOWER COLOR: Each of the gardens in this book is color-coordinated. Whether it is for a devotional garden or a bold summer garden, each plan underscores the importance of combining flowers of complementary colors. Even single-colored gardens follow this pattern, with white or gray gardens improved with a light touch of pink- or blue-flowering plants mixed in.

During the growing season, rely on annuals to keep the garden colorful while your perennials come in and out of bloom. Include annual and perennial species with unusual or variegated foliage to provide visual interest when other plants are not blooming.

SIZE: Height is important in every garden plan too. Short plants are best at the garden's edge; tall plants are better for background color and foliage. Let midsize perennials and annuals mingle in the center of the garden. Always read the plant label if you're unsure of how tall a particular plant will grow.

COLORFUL FOLIAGE: Annuals and perennials with silver or gray leaves are used in many of these garden plans. Artemisia, lavender, lavender cotton, and lamb's-ears provide a visual break from their more colorful cousins and look good when other flowers have faded.

CONTRAST: Plants with white flowers, such as nicotiana, moonflower, and jasmine, are another option if you want to provide contrast for brightly colored flowers. As a bonus, many white-flowering annuals and perennials are fragrant, releasing their sweet perfume after the sun goes down.

NEIGHBORING PLANTS: Plans in this book avoid invasive plants that spread quickly and overtake their neighbors. Gooseneck loosestrife, mints, including lemon balm and bee balm, violets, and ornamental ribbon grass are just a few of the species that will take over if you don't keep them in check.

If invasive plants grow near the site of your new garden, take steps to keep them out. A 9-inch strip of clear plastic carpet runner makes a good barrier (a typical 27-inch-wide runner can be cut into three 9-inch-wide strips). Dig a 7-inch-deep trench between the plants and the bed. Lean the runner against one side of the trench, leaving 2 inches above ground. Fill in the trench.

Planning is essential if you want a colorful garden in the late summer and fall. This autumn border contains goldenrod, aster, sedum, and black-eyed Susan.

PLANNING THE PERFECT BORDER

The Hot and Bright Garden (featured on pages 32 and 33) is an excellent example of how to design a beautiful flower garden. First, it effectively combines roses, annuals, and perennials in one bed. With a broad mix of different types of flowers, the garden is more likely to stay in bloom for a long period of time.

It's also composed primarily of red-, yellow-, and orange-flowering plants with only a clump of blue salvia at one end for relief and contrast (a gray-leaved plant such as artemisia or lamb's-ears would have also worked well here). This blending of colors from the red side of the spectrum is an effective way to create a bold border that's not overwhelming to the eye.

Height plays an important role here as well. Taller plants such as black-eyed Susan, yarrow, and daylily are planted at the back of the border with a tree rose adding height and visual interest. Shorter plants such as coreopsis, blanket flower, and dwarf dahlias bloom in front. In between the two extremes you find midsized plants: marguerite, butterfly weed, roses, sundrops, and penstemon.

Finally, notice the number of plants in each grouping. Instead of being lined up single file like toy soldiers, they are packed together in large, irregularly shaped groups. The clump of black-eyed Susan, for example, is made up of 13 plants. Specimen plants such as the tree roses are used sparingly as focal points. A focal point is an important component of every border because it attracts the eye and gives the design consistency and coherence.

SEASONAL GARDENS

Every gardener dreams of having a garden that's in full bloom from early spring to late fall. Without careful planning, you may end up with a garden that fades as the season progresses. One of the best ways to ensure year-round color is to plan for the seasons separately, then blend elements of each together as you plant.

It's also smart to include a mix of herbs, bulbs, flowering shrubs and trees, annuals, and perennial flowers. By including a variety of plants, you'll increase the odds that there will always be something colorful in your garden. In this chapter, you'll learn how to plan and plant beautiful gardens that will shine during each season of the year.

Planning is the key to having a garden that looks good in any season. Choose plants that complement one another in height, color, and bloom time. In this midsummer border, orange 'Enchantment' lily and 'Coronation Gold' yarrow erupt in a symphony of orange and yellow blooms. This color combination is typical of summer gardens. Spring gardens are generally pastel in nature, with blue-, pink-, and white-flowering perennials in the majority. By fall, most borders begin to mellow with flowers that develop bronze, golden, purple, and russet blooms. During the winter most gardens are more monochromatic but still show flashes of color with rose hips, grasses, and seed heads.

A SPRING GARDEN

The season of nature's reawakening, spring decks a garden in the year's first display of floral magnificence. Flowering shrubs, perennials, and bulbs are the mainstays of the spring garden. From modest beginnings—a scattering of winter aconite or crocuses, a sweep of daffodils, or a fanfare of tulips—a spring flower garden reaches a crescendo in most zones in April or May.

Though this garden is at its fullest in late spring, there is something of interest blooming throughout the season. Early-spring color is provided by lily-of-the-valley, forget-me-not, candytuft, cut-leaf lilac, and slender deutzia. Mid- to late-spring color is offered by the other perennials:

A meandering bark-covered path is an excellent low-maintenance choice for an informal spring perennial and bulb garden.

beautybush, spirea, and 'Constance Spry' rose.

The plants in the main list are appropriate for gardens in Zones 7 and 8 and the colder parts of Zone 9. Gardeners in Zones 4, 5, and 6 should choose a 'Raubritter' rose from the alternative list, rather than the less cold-tolerant 'Constance Spry'. Gardeners in Sunbelt Zone 9 and arid Zone 10 should plant the other recommended alternatives.

This spring garden needs a reasonably sunny spot. Locate it where it will receive at least six hours of sun each day during the period the plants are in bloom. The plants can take more shade afterwards, so a site that's partly shaded when the trees leaf out is fine. Give the plants routine garden watering.

Maintenance starts in late winter or early spring, when you should remove dead leaves and stems from the previous year. Deciduous shrubs flower on wood formed the previous year, so prune to remove old wood only after flowering. Thin out old wood on the climbing rose at the end of the dormant season, and train new growth as it matures over the summer. As the large perennials finish blooming, remove the spent flower stems or spikes. Be sure to cut off the spent blooms of Jupiter's beard, especially in mild-winter regions: Volunteer seedlings can become a nuisance. Most of the perennials will need replacing or dividing and replanting at some time. Lily-of-the-valley and peony can remain in place indefinitely. Daylily and Siberian iris need only infrequent dividing and replanting; bearded iris needs dividing every three to four years. Foxglove, fragrant daphne, columbine, and Jupiter's beard will need replacing as the old plants start to decline in vigor and productivity. In the warm zones (8, 9, and 10), they may last three or four years; in colder zones they may last no more than two.

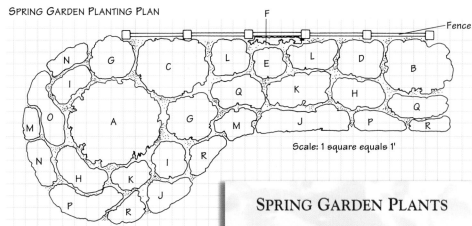

SPRING GARDEN PLANTING PLAN

Fence

Scale: 1 square equals 1'

Basket-of-gold and candytuft also will need replacing after several years, though shearing them back after bloom will keep them looking fresh. The forget-me-not will need replacing every two or three years, but volunteer seedlings usually ensure that there's always a new crop coming along.

VARIATIONS

In keeping with the newness of the season, the flower colors in this garden are clear and soft; bright, assertive tones are more the province of summer. You can vary the colors of the scheme by selecting different cultivars of peony, climbing rose, and bearded iris (some of which are decidedly assertive in color). Jupiter's beard is available in three colors: white, dusty rose, and light crimson. Initially, the shrubs—particularly the beautybush and cut-leaf lilac—will not fill the areas indicated in the planting scheme. To achieve a fuller appearance in the early years and to cover otherwise bare earth, enlarge the areas allotted to the neighboring perennials. Later, as the shrubs grow, you can gradually reduce the number of perennials.

The shape of this spring garden can be changed easily. To extend the length, place more of the shrubs at intervals along the fence line, fronting and interspersing them with more of the perennials. Or plant two of each shrub, spacing the second so that it is two-thirds the plant's diameter from the first; then stretch the length of each drift of perennials or add more drifts, following the patterns indicated in the plan. To shorten the bed, start the planting to the right of the large drift of candytuft, then plant drifts of forget-me-not or basket-of-gold, or both, to the right of the lupine and foxglove.

SPRING GARDEN PLANTS

A–1–Beautybush (Kolkwitzia amabilis)
B–1–Cut-leaf lilac (Syringa × laciniata)
C–1–Mockorange (Philadelphus virginalis 'Glacier')
D–1–Slender deutzia (Deutzia gracilis)
E–1–Spirea (Spiraea trilobata 'Fairy Queen')
F–1–'Constance Spry' rose
G–2–Peony (Paeonia lactiflora 'Festiva Maxima')
H–7–'Victoria Falls' bearded iris
I–6–'Ego' Siberian iris
J–8–Candytuft (Iberis sempervirens)
K–10–Fragrant daphne (Daphne odora 'Variegata')
L–10–Foxglove (Digitalis purpurea)
M–7–Daylily (Hemerocallis 'Stella de Oro')
N–18–Lily-of-the-valley (Convallaria majalis)
O–10–'McKenna Hybrids' columbine (Aquilegia)
P–19–Forget-me-not (Myosotis scorpioides)
Q–7–Jupiter's beard (Centranthus ruber)
R–12–Basket-of-gold (Aurinia saxatilis)

ALTERNATIVE SELECTIONS
A–1–Indian hawthorn (Rhaphiolepis indica 'Enchantress')
C–1–Rock rose (Cistus × 'Brilliancy')
D–1–Rock rose (Cistus skanbergii)
F–1–'Raubritter' rose for Zones 4, 5, and 6

A reliable spring bloomer, columbine comes in a wide variety of colors and bicolors and thrives in partially shady locations. Plants will often self-sow and spread through the garden.

A SUMMER GARDEN

At the height of summer, annual and perennial flowers are in full glory. Enjoy the show from a bench nestled in the floral finery. The bench also acts as a visual center of interest in your garden.

Summer brings the fullness of the gardening year; it's in this season that the greatest number of plants develop flowers in abundance. Summer also brings the warmest weather, signaling a time to take it easy (after you've attended to the watering) and enjoy the fruits of your gardening labors. This summer garden, therefore, features a shaded nook where you can sit, relax, and survey a riot of different flowers.

The shrubs and perennials in this summer border will thrive in Zones 5 through 9 and dry-summer Zone 10. All flower over a long period, some beginning in spring, others starting in summer and continuing into fall. The roses will provide color in all three seasons. Shrubs and perennials were chosen for this plan because of their relative permanence and lower maintenance needs. They will flower year after year, except dusty miller, which will need replacing each spring in Zones 5, 6, and 7. For this garden there are two lists of alternative selections. The first lists shrubs and perennials that are especially suited to mild winters in the warmer part of Zone 9 and Zone 10. The second group features a set of summer annuals distributed through the framework of shrubs and perennials. All the annuals must be planted anew every spring—an opportunity for enthusiastic gardeners to vary the planting each year with new colors and varieties.

A cool green hemlock hedge forms the backdrop in the illustration, though a wall or fence could instead provide an attractive background. The main plant list and the first list of alternatives include hedging shrubs that you should consider optional. If you choose to plant a hedge, remember to allow space for it to broaden beyond the confines of the bed.

Although the hedge, fence, or wall on three sides will shade this garden a little each day, this is a full-sun planting. Each part of the garden should have at least six hours of daily sun during the growing season. The plants need routine garden watering.

In late winter or early spring, prune and thin the vines and shrubs (except for the smoke tree) to keep them shapely and productive. Clean out the dead stems and leaves of the perennials and remove the spent annuals. Divide and replant any perennials that are overcrowded. During the summer bloom season, cut back the spent flower spikes of delphinium and beard-tongue; this will encourage a second flowering.

VARIATIONS

The predominant colors in this summer garden are pink, yellow, white, and blue—bright but not strident. For hot colors such as orange, red, and bronze, choose different cultivars of the shrub roses, rose of Sharon, bush cinquefoil, daylily, and coreopsis. Or select bright-colored annuals from the second list of alternatives.

If a double border is too elaborate for your space, you can plant either border as a rectangular bed facing a lawn or pathway. To do that, continue the front line to the back wall, past either the smoke tree (on left) or rose of Sharon (right); finish off the front of the border with narrow drifts of coreopsis, catmint, or both. To make one long border, rotate the right-hand border so that it extends the left one, abutting the two 'Pink Meidiland' roses and eliminating the plants that overlap in the superimposition. This will give you an impressive bed 40 to 45 feet long, with the smoke tree at one end of the planting and the rose of Sharon and 'Ballerina' rose at the other.

Once bee balm is established, it requires little care. It's popular with birds and butterflies and is available in a variety of colors and sizes. Plant in full sun.

SUMMER GARDEN PLANTS

A–1–Purple smoke tree (*Cotinus coggygria* 'Royal Purple')
B–1–Rose of Sharon (*Hibiscus syriacus* 'Diana')
C–1–Jackman clematis (*Clematis × jackmanii*). trained on trellis
D–18–Hedge: Canadian hemlock (*Tsuga canadensis*) planted 4 feet apart
E–2–'Pink Meidiland' rose
F–1–'Ballerina' rose
G–2–Bush cinquefoil (*Potentilla fruticosa* 'Katherine Dykes')
H–5–Bluebeard (*Caryopteris × clandonensis*)
I–15–'Pacific Giant Hybrids' delphinium
J–11–Fern-leaf yarrow (*Achillea filipendulina* 'Coronation Gold')
K–5–Shasta daisy (*Leucanthemum × superbum* 'Alaska')
L–6–Shasta daisy (*Leucanthemum × superbum* 'Snow Lady')
M–4–Russian sage (*Perovskia atriplicifolia*)
N–6–Baby's breath (*Gypsophila paniculata* 'Viette's Dwarf')
O–20–Beard-tongue (*Penstemon barbatus*)
P–8–Threadleaf coreopsis (*Coreopsis verticillata* 'Moonbeam')
Q–8–Daylily (*Hemerocallis* 'Winning Ways')
R–4–Spirea (*Spiraea japonica* 'Anthony Waterer')
S–10–Catmint (*Nepeta × faassenii*)
T–3–Cranesbill (*Geranium endressii* 'Wargrave Pink')
U–9–Lamb's-ears (*Stachys byzantina* 'Silver Carpet')
V–8–Dusty miller (*Senecio cineraria*)

ALTERNATIVE SELECTIONS I (FOR WARM REGIONS)
B–1–Oleander (*Nerium oleander*)
C–1–Jasmine (*Jasminum grandiflorum*)
D–18–Yaupon (*Ilex vomitoria*) or yew-pine (*Podocarpus macrophyllus*)
G–2–African lily (*Agapanthus orientalis*)
H–5–Marguerite (*Argyranthemum frutescens*)

ALTERNATIVE SELECTIONS II (ANNUALS)
L–6–Vinca (*Catharanthus roseus*)
R–4–Flowering tobacco (*Nicotiana alata*)
S–10–Garden verbena (*Verbena × hybrida*)
T–3–Plume cockscomb (*Celosia cristata*)

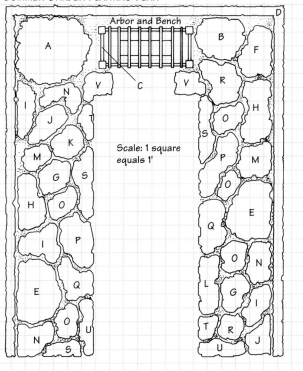

SUMMER GARDEN PLANTING PLAN

Arbor and Bench

Scale: 1 square equals 1'

A SUMMER ORNAMENTAL EDIBLE GARDEN

A stroll up two steps and down the path leads you to the front door of author and lecturer Rosalind Creasy, noted proponent of ornamental edible gardens. Although plants grown strictly for flowers predominate in this summer entryway garden (pictured on the cover of this book), a close look reveals several edibles tucked into the planting scheme: sweet peppers, rhubarb chard, and oriental bunching onions for cooking or salads; chives; two kinds of thyme; chamomile for tea; and nasturtiums for garnishes and salads.

From mid-spring through summer, this double border presents a colorful welcome. In this dry-summer Zone 9 garden, the vanguards of bloom are pansies, nasturtiums, and chives, closely followed by lobelia and sweet alyssum. By early summer nearly all the plants are either showing color or are in full flower. Overhead, the lightweight arbor that ties the two borders together is entwined with blue dawn flower, snail vine, and hops. Good soil, regular watering by drip irrigation, and full sun make this garden a winner. You can expect similar success in dry-summer Zones 8 and 10; for Zones 6 and 7 and moist-summer Zones 8 and 9, choose plants from the alternative selections.

Maintenance begins in late fall with a little cleanup. Remove spent stems of the perennials and played-out annuals and vegetables. In late winter, just before the growing season, clear out the dead foliage and stems of the vines, sedum, cranesbill, and dahlias. Cut back to the ground the stems of florist's chrysanthemum, Shasta daisy, obedient plant, and oregano. Reduce both the hybrid penstemon and beard-tongue to a few inches, and cut back nearly all growth on the catmint. Cut back the English lavender and 'Showbiz' rose by about half. In late winter or early spring, start thinking about the annuals. Set out pansy plants while the weather is cool; and plant nasturtium seeds and plants of lobelia, sweet alyssum, 'Lemon Gem' marigold, and sweet peppers when the soil has completely warmed.

After several years, you'll need to replace the perennials or dig them up and divide them. When these plants start to decline, replace them: rhubarb chard, penstemon, beard-tongue, slipper flower, lemon and silver thyme, and twinspur. When these plants start to decline, dig them up and divide them: Shasta daisy, florist's chrysanthemum, dahlia, sedum, obedient plant, hen and chicks, and catmint.

As colorful as it is good-looking, 'Purple Opal' basil makes a brilliant companion for other herbs such as dill, fennel, or oregano.

SUMMER ORNAMENTAL EDIBLE GARDEN PLANTING PLAN, Adapted from a garden designed by Rosalind Creasy

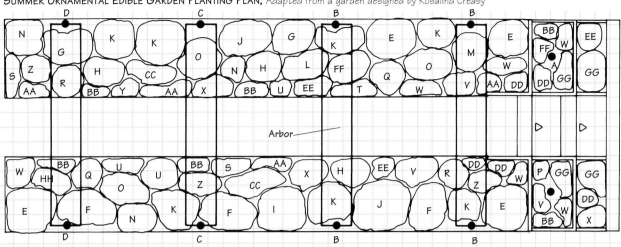

Arbor

Scale: 1 square equals 1'

VARIATIONS

In this garden, the visitor ascends steps between raised beds to reach the level path bounded by the long, narrow borders. For a level or gently sloping site, you can eliminate the raised beds that contain the standard roses; this will give you a shorter double border.

A garden composed entirely of herbs can be as colorful and fragrant as a full-scale flower border. Lavender cotton, parsley, basil, and dill are an unbeatable combination.

ORNAMENTAL EDIBLE-GARDEN PLANTS

A–2–'Showbiz' rose, as a 36-inch standard

B–4–Morning glory (Ipomoea tricolor 'heavenly Blue')

C–2–European hop (Humulus lupulus)

D–2–Japanese star jasmine (Trachelospermum asiaticum)

E–4–English lavender (Lavandula angustifolia)

F–15–Shasta daisy (Leucanthemum × superbum)

G–6–Florist's chrysanthemum (Dendranthema × grandiflorum)

H–8–'Autumn Joy' sedum

I–1–Dahlia, informal decorative hybrid

J–5–Oregano (Origanum laevigatum 'Hopleys')

K–16–Hybrid penstemon

L–3–Beard-tongue (Penstemon barbatus)

M–1–Dwarf pomegranate (Punica granatum 'Nana')

N–3–Obedient plant (Physostegia virginiana 'Summer Snow')

O–6–Slipper flower (Calceolaria integrifolia)

P–2–Hen and chicks (Sempervirens tectorum)

Q–2–Lemon thyme (Thymus × citriodorus)

R–2–Silver thyme (Thymus vulgaris 'Argenteus')

S–4–Twinspur (Diascia 'Ruby Fields')

T–2–Chamomile (Chamaemelum nobile)

U–5–Chives (Allium schoenoprasum)

V–4–Cranesbill (Geranium 'Johnson's Blue')

W–12–Moss verbena (Verbena tenuisecta)

X–3–Catmint (Nepeta × faassenii)

Y–2–Pansy (Viola × wittrockiana)

Z–8–Rhubarb chard (Beta vulgaris cicla 'Rhubarb')

AA–12–Lobelia (Lobelia erinus 'Crystal Palace')

BB–12–Sweet alyssum (Lobularia maritima)

CC–7–Sweet pepper (Capsicum annuum)

DD–8–Garden nasturtium, dwarf (Tropaeolum majus)

EE–4–Signet marigold (Tagetes tenuifolia 'Lemon Gem')

FF–5–Dahlia, bedding type

GG–10–Old-fashioned petunia (Petunia integrifolia)

HH–8–Green onion (Allium fistulosum)

ALTERNATIVE SELECTIONS

B–4–Morning glory (Ipomoea tricolor)

D–2–Scarlet runner bean (Phaseolus coccineus)

E–4–Bluebeard (Caryopteris × clandonensis)

M–1–Bush cinquefoil (Potentilla fruticosa 'Gold Drop')

O–6–Yarrow (Achillea 'Moonshine')

P–2–Hen and chicks (Echeveria hybrids)

S–4–Coral bells (Heuchera sanguinea)

W–12–Dalmatian bellflower (Campanula portenschlagiana)

A FALL GARDEN

To prevent a garden from fading in late summer, plant late-blooming perennials like these black-eyed Susans, and 'Autumn Joy' sedum and ornamental grasses .

In regions where seasons are distinct, fall heralds the close of the growing season. The last crops are ready for harvest, foliage changes to brilliant colors, and berries that will provide winter food for wildlife start to ripen. Yet fall also provides a final burst of flowers as an encore to summer's heady displays. As sure as the season gives us football, it also brings on chrysanthemums and the other daisy relatives, including a selected form of that sometimes weed, goldenrod.

This fall planting mingles all the colorful elements of the season. Vibrant red autumn foliage accompanies flowers in complementary yellow and bronze tones plus contrasting shades of blue and white; the European cranberrybush provides bright red fruits. Flowering begins in late summer and continues into November or until frost. The plants in the main list are for gardens in Zones 4 through 9. For gardens in Zones 3 and 10, use the appropriate alternative selection. Plants in all three lists need full sun and normal garden watering.

In mild-winter zones, you can get a head start on maintenance by removing spent flower stems during the winter. With the perennials trimmed back, the garden will have a neater appearance. In colder regions, especially where snow blurs the outlines of the plantings, begin maintenance in late winter or early spring. After you've tidied up dead leaves and anemone stems and removed the dead plants of the annual kochia, cut back the chrysanthemums, asters, boltonia, and goldenrod. If the perennials are losing vigor, divide and reset them just after the new growth begins. Spring is also the time to replace plants. Once the soil starts to warm, set out new cushion-type chrysanthemums, which may be short-lived in Zones 4, 5, and 6.

VARIATIONS

The simplest variations to this garden come from changing the color scheme. Choose from among a wide range of chrysanthemum

FALL GARDEN PLANTING PLAN

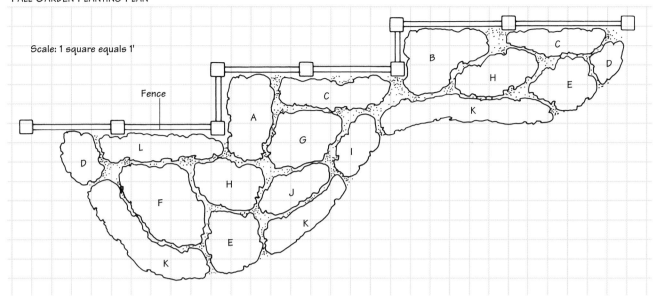

Scale: 1 square equals 1'

Fence

colors, pink Japanese anemones in addition to white ones, and asters that are white, blue-purple, or pink-red instead of just blue. All of these autumn bloomers are hardy enough to withstand a light frost and still remain colorful.

For a change in shape, consider creating a nearly round garden. Eliminating the right-hand segment of the plan leaves a near-semicircle. Sketch this part of the plan and you'll find that its mirror image, rotated 180 degrees, interlocks with the main plan to form a near-circular bed.

Mum's the word when it comes to fall color. Bold mums, asters, sedums, and grasses create a tapestry of bloom. Even after frost, the garden remains richly hued.

FALL GARDEN PLANTS

A–2–European cranberrybush (Viburnum opulus 'Compactum')
B–2–Dwarf burning bush (Euonymus alatus 'Compactus')
C–10–Goldenrod (Solidago 'Peter Pan')
D–3–Spirea (Spiraea japonica 'Goldflame')
E–8–Michaelmas daisy (Aster novi-belgii, dwarf varieties)
F–6–Japanese anemone (Anemone hybrida 'Honorine Jobert')
G–2– Michaelmas daisy (Aster novi-belgii, tall varieties)
H–6–Boltonia (Boltonia asteroides 'Snowbank')
I–1–Japanese barberry (Berberis thunbergii 'Crimson Pygmy')
J–3–'Autumn Joy' sedum
K–26–Chrysanthemum, cushion-mum type in bronze, yellow, or cream
L–7–Maiden grass (Miscanthus sinensis 'Morning Light')

ALTERNATIVE SELECTIONS, ZONE 3
A–2–American cranberrybush (Viburnum trilobum 'Compactum')
B–2–Redtwig dogwood (Cornus alba 'Sibirica')
I–4–Michaelmas daisy (Aster novi-belgii, dwarf variety)

ALTERNATIVE SELECTIONS, ZONE 10
B–3–Maiden grass (Miscanthus sinensis 'Gracillimus')
D–6–Golden marguerite (Anthemis tinctoria 'Moonlight')
I–3–Japanese blood grass (Imperata cylindrica 'Rubra')

A WINTER GARDEN

Keep winter interest in your garden by leaving the seed heads of annual and perennial flowers intact.

Despite the phrase "dead of winter," the season can offer color—even flower color. The catch is, it depends on where you live. In northern and mountain regions, where winter means a steady blanket of snow, garden color in winter is a sometimes thing, chiefly derived from evergreens, berried deciduous shrubs (before birds strip them), and the bright bark of certain dogwoods and willows. By contrast, gardeners in Zone 10 and the warmer parts of Zone 9 can plan for colorful flowers that will reliably enliven this least active but far-from-dead season. Between these two extremes lie the regions where snow may or may not occur, comes and goes, or arrives late and leaves early.

The planting scheme for this winter garden was designed for Zones 6 through 8, especially the Northeast, eastern seaboard, upper South, and Pacific Northwest. Winter-blooming heaths and Christmas rose carry the banner of flower color in white and pink. The dogwood and Japanese maple present colorful stems and bark, while the European cranberrybush offers striking clusters of red berries on leafless branches that attract colorful songbirds all winter long. The cliff green, juniper, and arborvitae contribute foliage—respectively, bronze, purplish, and golden.

The alternative plant selections are appropriate for Zone 9 and also for most gardens in Zone 8. The warmer climate allows an expanded range of flowering plants: Lenten rose, viola, primrose, bergenia, and camellia. The alternative scheme retains the Japanese maple for its coral-red stems and bark, which are a standout. Foliage color derives from the dwarf heavenly bamboo and the dwarf golden arborvitae.

The main planting needs sun for at least six hours each day. To satisfy the heaths, the soil must be well-drained and moisture-retentive.

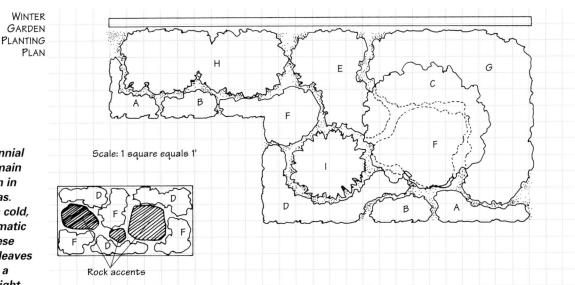

WINTER
GARDEN
PLANTING
PLAN

Scale: 1 square equals 1'

Many perennial flowers remain green, even in snowy areas. During this cold, monochromatic season, these few green leaves are always a welcome sight for gardeners.

Rock accents

WINTER GARDEN PLANTS

A–9–Cliff green (*Paxistima canbyi*)
B–9–Christmas rose (*Helleborus niger*)
C–1–Japanese maple (*Acer palmatum* 'Sango-kaku')
D–9–Heath (*Erica carnea* 'Springwood') (15 in variation bed)
E–5–Creeping juniper (*Juniperus horizontalis* 'Plumosa')
F–14–Heath (*Erica carnea* 'Winter Beauty') (19 in variation bed)
G–3–European cranberrybush (*Viburnum opulus* 'Compactum')
H–2–Redtwig dogwood (*Cornus alba* 'Sibirica')
I–1–American arborvitae (*Thuja occidentalis* 'Rheingold')

ALTERNATIVE SELECTIONS
A–11–Lenten rose (*Helleborus orientalis*)
B–19–Viola (*Viola cornuta*)
D–24–Polyanthus primrose (*Primula × polyantha*) (52 in variation bed)
E–10–Dwarf heavenly bamboo (*Nandina domestica* 'Harbor Dwarf')
F–19–Leather bergenia (*Bergenia crassifolia*) (31 in alternative bed)
H–2–Japanese camellia (*Camellia japonica* 'C.M. Wilson' or 'Pink Perfection')
I–1–Arborvitae (*Thuja occidentalis* 'Rheingold')

The alternative planting needs partial shade or filtered sunlight for about half the day to accommodate the camellias and Lenten rose.

Minimal maintenance is a bonus with this planting. In fall, after the leaves have dropped, rake off the ones that cover the low plants. In spring, clean out all unsightly and dead foliage on the perennials. After the heaths have stopped flowering, shear off the spent stems to keep the plants dense and compact. In the alternative planting, you will need to replace the violas each year in fall, but they may also spread on their own. Although the primroses are perennials,

in the warmest areas you will get the best display by setting out new plants each fall.

ALTERNATIVE DESIGN

This variation is deliberately small— a fragment of color to cherish during the winter. The square island bed is optional. As shown, it features a moorland patch of heaths and rock. However, it could just as easily contain a bench nestled among heaths (or Lenten rose and primroses), a place to contemplate these special winter-time offerings.

A THREE-SEASON GARDEN

Roses, catmint, and lamb's-ears are plants you can depend on for spring-till-fall color. Even when they are not in bloom, their foliage is attractive.

For a garden that will appeal throughout the growing season, consider this three-season scheme that provides color from spring into fall. Although the color may not at all times match the intense color found in the spring garden or the summer gardens, this planting definitely doesn't fall short in either beauty or interest. Here, you will be especially aware of the attractiveness of the individual plants and the pleasing associations of foliage and flowers.

All plants in this scheme were chosen for their long period of bloom (the roses, in fact, are varieties that flower in all three seasons). Rather than bursts and gaps of blossoms, there will be a flowering continuum. The backbone of the garden is formed by shrubs chosen for their foliage as much as for their flowers. Perennials make up the remainder of the scheme, though the alternative selections list suggests three long-blooming annuals that you could substitute for some of the foreground drifts. Plants in the main list thrive in Zones 5 through 9, although in Zones 5 and 6 the floribunda roses will need winter protection and the beard-tongue may need replacing every two or three years. With the substitutions in the alternatives list, the planting will succeed in the dry-summer regions of Zone 10. In all zones, locate the planting in full sun and give it routine garden watering.

Late winter and early spring are the times to perform basic maintenance. Prune roses, rose

THREE-SEASON PLANTING PLAN

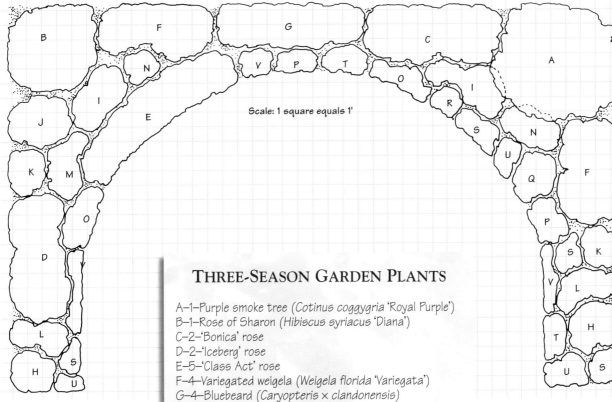

Scale: 1 square equals 1'

THREE-SEASON GARDEN PLANTS

A–1–Purple smoke tree (Cotinus coggygria 'Royal Purple')
B–1–Rose of Sharon (Hibiscus syriacus 'Diana')
C–2–'Bonica' rose
D–2–'Iceberg' rose
E–5–'Class Act' rose
F–4–Variegated weigela (Weigela florida 'Variegata')
G–4–Bluebeard (Caryopteris × clandonensis)
H–2–Japanese barberry (Berberis thunbergii 'Atropurpurea')
I–6–Russian sage (Perovskia atriplicifolia)
J–2–Boltonia (Boltonia asteroides 'Snowbank')
K–6–Michaelmas daisy (Aster novi-belgii, tall blue cultivar)
L–6–Yarrow (Achillea ageratum 'W.B. Child')
M–5–Fern-leaf yarrow (Achillea filipendulina 'Coronation Gold')
N–7–False sunflower (Heliopsis helianthoides 'Summer Sun')
O–6–Threadleaf coreopsis (Coreopsis verticillata 'Moonbeam')
P–5–'Autumn Joy' sedum
Q–4–Daylily (Hemerocallis 'Evergold')
R–3–Daylily (Hemerocallis 'Stella de Oro')
S–14–Beard-tongue (Penstemon barbatus 'Prairie Fire')
T–9–Lamb's-ears (Stachys byzantina)
U–8–Leather bergenia (Bergenia crassifolia)
V–9–Catmint (Nepeta × faassenii)

ALTERNATIVE SELECTIONS (FOR ZONE 10)
B–1–Oleander (Nerium oleander 'Casablanca')
F–4–Tree germander (Teucrium fruticans)
G–4–Ox-eye daisy for (Leucanthemum vulgare)
H–2–Fortnight lily for (Dietes vegeta)
I–6–Glory bush (Tibouchina urvilleana)
N–7–Kafir lily (Clivia miniata)
P–16–French marigold (Tagetes patula)
T–9–Petunia (Petunia hybrida)
V–9–Vinca (Catharanthus roseus)

of Sharon, and bluebeard to shape and remove any unproductive wood. Cut back the perennials that send up flowering stems from clumps or woody bases, and remove any dead leaves. After the variegated weigela blooms, prune or thin as needed. Remove the spent rose blossom clusters when they become untidy.

VARIATIONS

Adding a promenade path at the front of the crescent design will provide a pleasant stroll as well as a possible focal point at the end of a garden. Another alternative is to cut the scheme in half. Split the bed at the bluebeard. Then the one side becomes a corner bed. Either half will fulfill the promise of three-season color.

Although it's a fall bloomer, 'Autumn Joy' sedum has handsome, fleshy blue-green leaves that look attractive in spring and summer. Sedum is an early riser in spring and makes an ideal companion for bulbs.

COLOR GARDENS

Before 1908 few gardeners thought much about color in the garden or about creating borders with single colors. But then, the famous English gardener Gertrude Jekyll published her book, Colour in the Flower Garden. This ground-breaking text outlined ways in which single-tone gardens could be planted as dramatic alternatives to the traditional mixed color border. Since then, gardeners around the world have embraced the concept by designing gardens that showcase variations of a single hue. In this chapter you'll find a selection of tasteful garden plans based on flower color.

Often the most dramatic beds and borders are those that include plants of similar color. This yellow perennial garden contains large drifts of black-eyed Susan, orange and cream daylilies, and white coneflower.

A WHITE GARDEN

A garden of white flowers has an undeniable romantic appeal. On a sunny day it is refreshing; in cloudy or foggy weather it is soft and luminous. And at night it becomes shadowy, ethereal, otherworldly: a setting out of *A Midsummer Night's Dream*.

Many so-called white gardens include flowers of pale cream, ice blue, and blush pink in addition to pure white. Except for the blue-flowered Russian sage, this planting scheme favors truly white blossoms, augmented by plants that have gray or silvery white foliage (some of which have insignificant flowers of yellow or blue). For a white-flowered substitute for the Russian sage, choose colewort from the alternative selections; it forms a 6-foot-tall cloud of tiny white flowers.

Although the greatest variety of flowers appears in summer, the plants bloom from spring into fall. During periods with few blooms, the foliage emphasizes the garden's overall whiteness.

This garden does best in Zones 7 and 8 and the colder parts of Zone 9. For gardens in Zones 5 and 6, plant the suggested alternative climbing rose and substitute lamb's-ears for lavender cotton. In Zones 9 or 10, substitute the other selections.

Locate the garden where it will receive six or more hours of sunlight a day during the growing season and water on a normal schedule. Because the planting includes shrubs, perennials, and annuals, maintenance is varied. The honeysuckle hedge shouldn't need regular trimming—it grows compact and hedgelike without shearing—but occasionally you may need to head back wayward growth. Each year in late winter, assess the other shrubs (roses, summersweet, European cranberrybush) and do whatever pruning is necessary to keep them shapely.

Late winter or early spring is also the time to tidy up the perennials, dividing and replanting, or replacing, any that have declined in vigor. Cut down last year's spent stems of those that die back each fall or winter. Head back by up to half the shrubby perennials, such as 'Powis Castle' artemisia and lavender cotton, to keep plants compact and leafy. When the soil has warmed, set out plants of the one annual—deliciously fragrant flowering tobacco.

To ensure the evergreen candytuft survives the winter in Zones 5 and 6, lightly cover the plants with cut evergreen boughs in late fall.

VARIATIONS

If this double-armed planting takes more space than you have available, consider making a rectangular bed 24 feet long by 8 feet wide. Select one arm of the design and drop the other, continuing the bed line across the paved area to the wall or fence. This reduces the paved seating area to a triangle but leaves enough room for a chair or small bench.

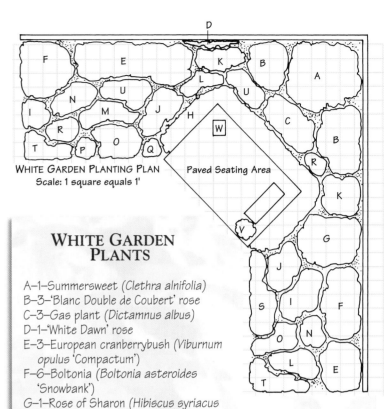

WHITE GARDEN PLANTING PLAN
Scale: 1 square equals 1'

Paved Seating Area

The snow white flowers of 'Iceberg' roses are a mainstay in many all-white gardens. This classic Modern rose produces lots of flowers and requires little care to stay in top form.

Lily-of-the-valley makes an ideal ground cover for partly shady locations. It sends up clusters of fragrant, bell-like flowers in early spring. It is an aggressive plant that spreads quickly.

WHITE GARDEN PLANTS

A–1–Summersweet (Clethra alnifolia)
B–3–'Blanc Double de Coubert' rose
C–3–Gas plant (Dictamnus albus)
D–1–'White Dawn' rose
E–3–European cranberrybush (Viburnum opulus 'Compactum')
F–6–Boltonia (Boltonia asteroides 'Snowbank')
G–1–Rose of Sharon (Hibiscus syriacus 'Diana')
H–12–Honeysuckle (Lonicera × xylosteoides 'Clavey's Dwarf')
I–3–Artemisia 'Powis Castle'
J–4–Baby's breath (Gypsophila paniculata 'Bristol Fairy')
K–5–Russian sage (Perovskia atriplicifolia)
L–3–Gardenia (Gardenia angusta)
M–6–Japanese anemone (Anemone hybrida 'Honorine Jobert')
N–7–Delphinium (Delphinium 'Galahad')
O–12–Shasta daisy (Leucanthemum × superbum 'Snow Lady')
P–1–Sedum (Sedum 'Frosty Morn')
Q–1–Siberian iris (Iris sibirica, 'Little White')
R–4–Siberian Iris (Iris sibirica, 'White Swirl')
S–4–Lavender cotton (Santolina chamaecyparissus)
T–10–Evergreen candytuft (Iberis sempervirens)
U–18–Flowering tobacco (Nicotiana alata)
V–1–Ox-eye daisy (Leucanthemum vulgare 'May Queen')
W–1–'Iceberg' rose as a standard, in container; alternative for statuary

ALTERNATIVE SELECTIONS (FOR ZONES 9 OR 10 EXCEPT WHERE NOTED)
A–1–Oleander (Nerium oleander)
C–3–Ox-eye daisy (Leucanthemum vulgare)
D–1–'Mme. Plantier' rose, for Zones 5 and 6
E–3–Tree germander (Teucrium fruticans)
G–1–Crimson-spot rock rose (Cistus ladanifer)
H–12–Variegated dwarf myrtle (Myrtus communis 'Compacta Variegata')
J–6–Yarrow (Achillea ptarmica 'The Pearl')
K–2–Colewort (Crambe cordifolia)
L–3–Peony (Paeonia lactiflora, white cultivar)
Q–1–Lily-of-the-Nile (Agapanthus 'Rancho White' or 'Peter Pan')
R–4–White lily-of-the-Nile (Agapanthus orientalis 'Albidus')
S–9–Lamb's-ears (Stachys byzantina 'Silver Carpet'), for Zones 5 and 6

A GARDEN OF COOL TONES

A garden of cool tones contains the essential elements of a white garden (see pages 26 and 27), but alters the mood by including flowers in shades of blue and violet. Although a purely white garden is cool and light—even bright in full sunlight—the addition of blue provides a shadowy element that registers "cool" even on the hottest days. A special moment occurs at twilight when the blues glow as though with light of their own.

Blue-flowering perennials such as lavender and catmint are good foils for brightly colored orange, red, and yellow flowers. In this garden lavender and catmint combine with yellow daylily.

This planting scheme provides an impressive floral display from late spring through late summer—the time of year you want to sit on the terrace and soak up the coolness. And there will be some flowers over an even longer period: magnolia in early spring and aster, sage, and roses in fall. The main planting serves gardens in Zones 5 through 9; the alternative selections extend the scheme into the dry-summer part of Zone 10, although these plants will thrive in Zone 9 as well.

All but one of the plants appreciate full sun: a minimum of six hours per day. The exception—

the bigleaf hydrangea—prefers a half day of sun where summers are hot, or dappled or filtered sunlight throughout the day. As it gains height, the magnolia will eventually shade and protect the bigleaf hydrangea.

Late winter or early spring, weather permitting, is the time to undertake major garden maintenance. Most shrubs (except the magnolia, cinquefoil, and germander) will need regular pruning: the roses merely trimmed to shape, the English lavender and hydrangea cut back to about half, the common butterfly bush and bluebeard cut back to about 12 inches. Tidy up the perennials, removing dead leaves and last year's spent stems. Cut back the lavender cotton and artemisia by one-half to two-thirds to keep them compact. Cut back the catmint, Russian sage, and Mexican bush sage nearly to the ground. In time, most of the perennials will need dividing and replanting. Do this while the plants are still dormant.

COOL-TONES GARDEN PLANTING PLAN

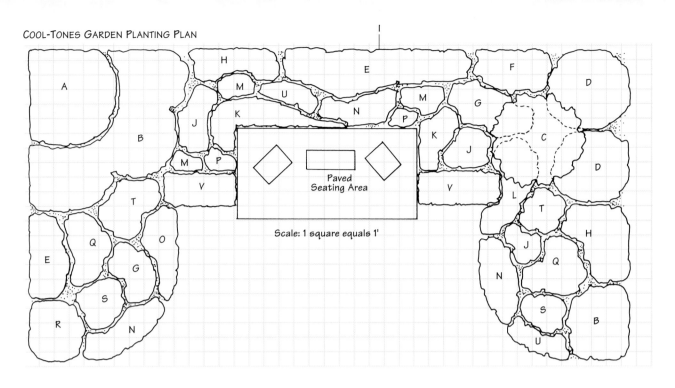

Paved
Seating Area

Scale: 1 square equals 1'

COOL-TONES GARDEN PLANTS

A–1–Common butterfly bush (*Buddleia davidii* 'Empire Blue' or other blue cultivar)
B–4–'Blanc Double de Coubert' rose
C–1–Magnolia (*Magnolia loebneri* 'Merrill')
D–2–Bigleaf hydrangea (*Hydrangea macrophylla* 'Tricolor')
E–6–Bluebeard (*Caryopteris × clandonensis*)
F–2–English lavender (*Lavandula angustifolia*)
G–9–Frikart's aster (*Aster frikartii*)
H–4–Colewort (*Crambe cordifolia*)
I–1–Clematis (*Clematis lanuginosa* 'Candida'), allowed to weave through planting
J–16–Perennial salvia (*Salvia × sylvestris* 'Maynight')
K–8–Snow-in-summer (*Cerastium tomentosum*)
L–7–Dalmatian bellflower (*Campanula portenschlagiana*)
M–13–Shasta daisy (*Leucanthemum × superbum*)
N–12–Catmint (*Nepeta × faassenii*)

O–4–Lavender cotton (*Santolina chamaecyparissus*)
P–4–Siberian Iris (*Iris sibirica*, 'White Swirl')
Q–6–White Jupiter's beard (*Centranthus ruber* 'Albus')
R–1–Cinquefoil (*Potentilla fruticosa* 'Abbotswood')
S–2–Rue (*Ruta graveolens* 'Jackman's Blue')
T–3–False indigo (*Baptisia australis*)
U–8–Lamb's-ears (*Stachys byzantina*)
V–8–Russian sage (*Perovskia atriplicifolia*)

ALTERNATIVE SELECTIONS
E–6–Tree germander (*Teucrium fruticans*)
H–6–Mexican bush sage (*Salvia leucantha*)
I–1–Potato vine (*Solanum jasminoides*)
R–1–Artemisia 'Powis Castle'
V–8–English lavender (*Lavandula angustifolia* 'Hidcote' or 'Munstead')

VARIATIONS

The size and shape of this planting can be changed in several ways. To create a rectangular garden, draw a line from one side of the plan to the other at the lower edge of the hedge, eliminating the plantings below this line. Extend the hedge to meet D and B. For a narrower scheme, select one arm of the design and eliminate the other. This leaves you with an L-shaped plan, the short arm containing the butterfly bush and three roses or hydrangeas.

Pink roses are especially beautiful when they are paired with silver and blue plants. Here lamb's-ears and catmint bloom nearby.

A PASTEL GARDEN

Apricot- and pink-flowering roses are a symphony of color when interplanted with pastel blue lily-of-the-Nile.

Colors and color associations affect the mood of a planting, as well as alter our perceptions of space. This garden, composed of pastel tones and tints, suggests springtime freshness. It also seems more distant and smaller than if it were planted with vibrant reds, yellows, and other equally attention-compelling colors. Set this planting into a sizable lawn, and the eye will be encouraged to look past it as well as at it. In a small garden the soft pastel colors give a sense of depth, whereas bright colors seem to foreshorten and shrink the space.

The assortment of shrubs and perennials in this garden will show color from mid-spring to early autumn, reaching a peak in early to midsummer. The several gray-foliaged plants contribute to the overall pastel tones and provide color throughout the growing season.

All plants on the main list except peony will prosper in Zones 5 to 9 if the site receives full sun. In Zone 8 to 9 replace peony with the alternative selection—white Jupiter's beard—and choose other alternative selections if you wish. In dry-summer Zone 10, use all the alternative selections.

Pruning and general cleanup in late winter or early spring constitute the major annual maintenance for this garden. Remove old, unproductive wood from the mockorange and rose, then prune only if you need to correct their shape or limit their size. Cut the Russian sage and catmint to the ground; cut back the English lavender by half. Most perennials will need dividing and replanting after three or four years. However, you many need to replace the beard-tongue, penstemon, mallow, and golden feverfew as frequently as every other year. These perennials may come back on their own, but they are not always reliable.

VARIATIONS

This kidney-shape bed was designed as an island planting to ornament an expanse of lawn. The low plants at the perimeter scale up to the two high points of mockorange and shrub rose. If you draw a line through the bed connecting the dots

PASTEL GARDEN
PLANTING PLAN

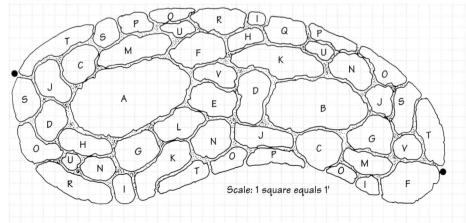

Scale: 1 square equals 1'

shown on either end of the plan, you will create two irregular beds, either of which you could place against a fence or wall. The half-oval bed will contain two high points: the shrub rose and the mockorange; the serpentine-edge bed will gain its height from the mockorange.

The key to a successful pastel garden is to select plants with complementary colors. For example, pink poppies, blue salvia, and silvery lamb's-ears provide a refreshing retreat during the early summer in this garden.

PASTEL GARDEN PLANTS

A–2–Mockorange (*Philadelphus virginalis* 'Minnesota Snowflake')
B–2–'Pink Meidiland' or 'Bonica' rose
C–2–Cinquefoil (*Potentilla* 'Katherine Dykes')
D–7–Russian sage (*Perovskia atriplicifolia*)
E–2–Common rose mallow (*Hibiscus moscheutos* 'Pink Charm')
F–2–Peony (*Paeonia lactiflora*, white cultivar)
G–4–Gas plant (*Dictamnus albus*)
H–7–Bee balm (*Monarda didyma* 'Croftway Pink')
I–4–Daylily (*Hemerocallis*, light yellow miniature cultivar)
J–8–Daylily (*Hemerocallis*, light pink cultivar)
K–14–Yarrow (*Achillea* 'Moonshine')
L–2–Baby's breath (*Gypsophila paniculata* 'Viette's Dwarf')
M–11–Beard-tongue (*Penstemon barbatus* 'Elfin Pink')
N–11–Frikart's aster (*Aster frikartii*)
O–12–Cranesbill (*Geranium endressii* 'Wargrave Pink')
P–9–Lamb's-ears (*Stachys byzantina*)
Q–2–Bloody cranesbill (*Geranium sanguineum*)
R–7–English lavender (*Lavandula angustifolia* 'Munstead')
S–9–Bee balm (*Monarda didyma* 'Marshall's Delight')
T–11–Catmint (*Nepeta x faassenii*)
U–5–Golden feverfew (*Tanacetum parthenium* 'Aureum')
V–7–Mallow (*Malva alcea var. fastigiata*)

ALTERNATIVE SELECTIONS
A–2–Common butterfly bush (*Buddleia davidii*, white cultivar)
C–2–Marguerite (*Argyranthemum frutescens*)
D–7–English lavender (*Lavandula angustifolia*)
F–4–White Jupiter's beard (*Centranthus ruber* 'Albus')
G–2–False indigo (*Baptisia australis*)
H–7–Purple coneflower (*Echinacea purpurea*, white cultivar)
L–1–'Powis Castle' Artemisia
M–11–Penstemon (*Penstemon hirsutus*)
Q–2–Dwarf cupflower (*Nierembergia caerula*)
S–6–Blue daisy (*Felicia amelloides*)

A HOT AND BRIGHT GARDEN

As spring grows into summer, the garden blooms in hotter colors—red, yellow, and orange. A tall green hedge cools down this hot-colored bed.

This bed fairly shouts, "Hey, look at me," though dark glasses might be in order. Red, orange, and yellow jostle for attention, punctuated by patches of vibrant purple. The perennials (and annuals on the alternative list) reach their brassy climax appropriately in summer and, weather permitting, will last into fall. Much of this brightness is provided by those mainstays of summer: members of the daisy family. Aside from the roses, which give color from spring into fall, all the plants are perennials. For a planting scheme that features summer annuals, use the list of alternative selections.

This vibrant garden bed needs as much sun as possible. Bright colors, sunshine, and summer warmth combine to create a scene that radiates. The main plant list is suitable for Zones 4 through 9 and dry-summer Zone 10. The alternative selections are annuals for the same zones, although the gazanias and blanket flowers may not be at their best where the summers are hot and wet.

In Zones 4 through 7, maintenance begins in fall, when you will need to protect the roses from lethal winter temperatures. The two standard roses are particularly vulnerable and will need special attention (see Ortho's *All About Roses*). In all zones, late winter or early spring is the time to prune roses, to remove weak and worn-out wood, and to shape the plants. Perennials should get an annual cleanup. Remove the dead leaves and spent stems in fall or in early spring before growth begins.

HOT AND BRIGHT GARDEN PLANTING PLAN

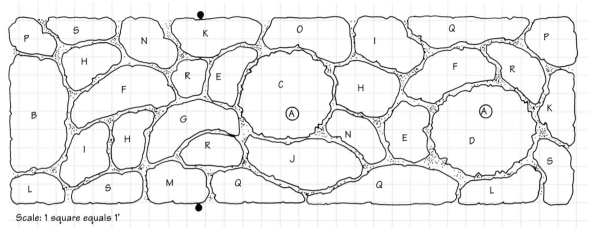

Scale: 1 square equals 1'

In Zones 4 through 7, you will need to replace the beard-tongues and dahlias each year; the other perennials will need dividing and replanting periodically as they become overcrowded.

VARIATIONS

You can cut the length of the bed by one-third if you draw a line between the two dots shown on the plan and eliminate all the plants in the smaller portion. The number of 'Goldfink' coreopsis will be cut to four, and the alternative purple scarlet sage will be cut to eight. To make a better edge where the line has shortened the bed, plant five blanket flowers instead of the butterfly weed, three evening primroses instead of the common yarrow, and four sage plants instead of the penstemon. If you are using the alternative list, substitute 12 French marigolds for the African marigolds, two zinnias for the common yarrow, and five gazanias for the penstemon.

HOT AND BRIGHT GARDEN PLANTS

A–2–'Redgold', standard rose ("tree")
B–3–'Europeana' rose
C–8–Daylily (Hemerocallis, yellow cultivar)
D–8–Daylily (Hemerocallis, red cultivar)
E–5–Butterfly weed (Asclepias tuberosa)
F–9–Fern-leaf yarrow (Achillea filipendulina 'Coronation Gold')
G–5–Common yarrow (Achillea millefolium 'Fire King')
H–13–Black-eyed Susan (Rudbeckia hirta)
I–4–Golden marguerite (Anthemis tinctoria 'Aureum')
J–5–Lanceleaf coreopsis (Coreopsis lanceolata)
K–7–Lanceleaf coreopsis (Coreopsis lanceolata 'Goldfink')
L–3–Threadleaf coreopsis (Coreopsis verticillata 'Zagreb')
M–3–Mouse ear coreopsis (Coreopsis auriculata 'Nana')
N–4–Common sneezeweed (Helenium autumnale 'Brilliant')
O–7–Blanket flower (Gaillardia grandiflora 'Baby Cole')
P–3–Sundrops (Oenothera fruticosa)
Q–10–Dahlia, bedding type, preferably red or orange flowers
R–9–Beard-tongue (Penstemon 'Pike's Peak Purple')
S–11–Sage (Salvia superba)

ALTERNATIVE SELECTIONS
E–13–African marigold (Tagetes erecta, yellow selection)
J–9–Zinnia (Zinnia grandiflora, orange selection)
K–15–Purple scarlet sage (Salvia splendens, purple selection)
L–7–Blanket flower (Gaillardia pulchella)
M–8–Gazania, yellow cultivar
N–12–Flowering tobacco (Nicotiana alata, red selection)
O–23–French marigold (Tagetes patula)
P–5–Zinnia (Zinnia angustifolia)
Q–14–Scarlet sage (Salvia splendens, red selection)
S–18–Gazania, orange cultivar

For the boldest effect, always plant in large clumps. These orange 'Enchantment' lilies and yellow false sunflower create a bright color show in June and July.

A COLORFUL FOLIAGE GARDEN

Plants with colorful foliage like these cannas, red-leaved dahlias, bananas, and ginger look good even when they're not in bloom.

Most gardens rely on flowers for color. This planting scheme gives a different color angle: your chance to say it with foliage. A few of the plants bear flowers, but the floral show is merely a dividend in a planting that is a colorful tapestry of leaves from spring through fall. One green-leaved plant—the wall germander—adds an exotic and colorful counterpoint to the reds, yellows, and grays.

With one exception, this planting will thrive in Zones 5 through 9, given well-drained soil and sun for at least six hours each day. The golden elderberry needs more winter chill than Zones 8 and 9 can offer. In these zones, choose silverberry from the alternative selections. Gardeners in dry-summer Zone 10 should choose all the alternative selections—
the silverberry instead of the golden

When shopping for perennials, look for varieties with variegated foliage. Sweet iris, for example, is a small-flowered iris with handsome striped leaves that are especially beautiful when the sun shines through them.

COLORFUL FOLIAGE GARDEN PLANTS

A–1–Purple smoke tree (Cotinus coggygria 'Royal Purple')
B–1–Vicary golden privet (Ligustrum × vicaryi)
C–1–Golden elderberry (Sambucus racemosa)
D–3–Russian sage (Perovskia atriplicifolia)
E–1–Adam's needle (Yucca filamentosa 'Gold Sword' or 'Bright Eagle')
F–1–Japanese barberry (Berberis thunbergii 'Atropurpurea')
G–6–English lavender (Lavandula angustifolia)
H–2–Rue (Ruta graveolens 'Jackman's Blue')
I–7–Japanese blood grass (Imperata cylindrica 'Rubra')
J–9–Lavender cotton (Santolina chamaecyparissus)
K–5–Wall germander (Teucrium chamaedrys)
L–8–Sedum (Sedum spurium 'Dragon's Blood')
M–5–Tricolor garden sage (Salvia officinalis 'Tricolor')
N–2–Maiden grass (Miscanthus sinensis)
O–4–Catmint (Nepeta × faassenii)
P–1–Spirea (Spiraea japonica 'Limemound')
Q–1–Variegated purple moor grass (Molinia caerulea 'Variegata')

ALTERNATIVE SELECTIONS
C–1–Silverberry (Elaeagnus pungens 'Maculata')
D–3–Dusty miller (Senecio viravira or S. cineraria 'Silver Dust')
F–1–Christmas tree kalanchoe (Kalanchoe laciniata)

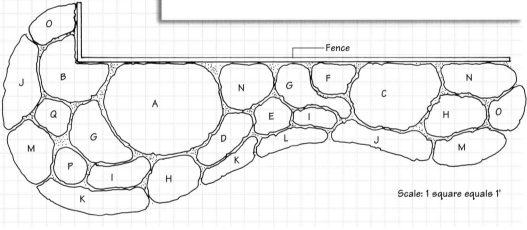

Scale: 1 square equals 1'

COLORFUL-FOLIAGE
PLANTING PLAN

elderberry, the dusty miller instead of the Russian sage, the kalanchoe instead of the Japanese barberry, and the golden feverfew instead of the spirea. The alternative selections can also be used in Zone 9.

Once-a-year maintenance should keep this planting presentable. In late winter or early spring, do some general cleanup and pruning. Cut back the Russian sage, catmint, and maiden grass to within a few inches of the ground. Cut back the English lavender and tricolor garden sage by about half to promote compact growth. As necessary—perhaps not yearly—cut back the lavender cotton and wall germander to keep them compact. Thin the oldest, most unproductive stems from the spirea; if necessary, prune to shape the Vicary golden privet and golden elderberry. After

several years, the sedum may start to become patchy. When this happens, fill in the bare spots with new cuttings, or replant entirely with new cuttings or plants. You can also dig and divide the old sedum plants to rejuvenate them. Even a small piece of stem will root and become a new plant.

VARIATIONS

For a smaller bed, you can use two-thirds of the plan, starting from the left, going as far as, and including, the Japanese barberry (F) but stopping short of the golden elderberry (C). If the back line needs to be straight, extend the existing back line to the edge of the bed, eliminating the catmint planting and one of the lavender cotton plants.

A GRAY GARDEN

Soothing, misty, and even ghostly, this gray garden features subtle contrasts of foliage tones, shapes, and textures. Leaves range in color from gray-green and silvery blue to almost white, and vary in shape from broad to narrow, from simple to filigree to spiky. Even the leaf surfaces play a part; some are furry and others are covered with a delicate powder. Depending on foliage and habit of growth, the effect varies from solid and bulky to intricately twiggy to feathery. All this subtle interplay makes for close-up viewing—and is best appreciated from an appropriately gray bench of concrete or weathered wood.

Despite a color scheme suggesting fog or overcast skies, this garden prefers sun for at least six hours a day. In hot-summer regions, though, the dogwood (and alternative hydrangea) will benefit from some afternoon shading by the Russian olive (or the alternative willow-leaved pear). Without sufficient shade, the dogwood and hydrangea will be the first shrubs to show signs of water stress. Most of the plants can survive with a little less water than normal, but they do need well-drained soil—especially the gray-leaved perennials, which may die in wet winter soils. The main-list plants thrive in Zones 6 through 8. In Zone 9 and dry-summer Zone 10, choose the alternative selections.

Late-winter or early-spring pruning should be a yearly maintenance ritual. Remove the old stems of the dogwood or hydrangea.

'Silver King' artemisia, almost bright enough to glow in the dark, grows 4 feet tall and requires little care. It can spread quickly.

GRAY GARDEN PLANTS

A–1–Russian olive (*Elaeagnus angustifolia*)
B–2–Variegated Tatarian dogwood (*Cornus alba* 'Elegantissima')
C–2–Sea buckthorn (*Hippophae rhamnoides*)
D–5–Bluebeard (*Caryopteris × clandonensis*)
E–1–Silverberry (*Elaeagnus pungens*)
F–3–Rue (*Ruta graveolens* 'Jackman's Blue')
G–4–Russian sage (*Perovskia atriplicifolia*)
H–7–English lavender (*Lavandula angustifolia*)
I–4–Globe thistle (*Echinops ritro*)
J–1–'Powis Castle' Artemisia
K–16–Lavender cotton (*Santolina chamaecyparissus*)
L–4–Iris, tall bearded hybrid 'Song of Norway'
M–8–Catmint (*Nepeta × faassenii*)
N–10–Blue fescue (*Festuca glauca*)
O–9–Blue oat grass (*Helictotrichon sempervirens*)
P–4–Lamb's-ears (*Stachys byzantina*)
Q–8–White campion (*Lychnis coronaria* 'Alba')
R–3–Beach wormwood (*Artemisia stellerana* 'Silver Brocade')
S–6–Snow-in-summer (*Cerastium tomentosum*)
T–Woolly thyme in paving (*Thymus pseudolanuginosus*) (number depends on paving pattern)

ALTERNATIVE SELECTIONS

A–1–Willow-leaved pear (*Pyrus salicifolia* 'Pendula')
B–2–Bigleaf hydrangea (*Hydrangea macrophylla* 'Tricolor')
C–2–Tree germander (*Teucrium fruticans*)
D–5–Bush morning glory (*Convolvulus cneorum*)
E–1–Japanese pittosporum (*Pittosporum tobira* 'Variegata')
G–3–Purple sage (*Salvia officianalis* 'Purpurascens')

Trim the remaining stems as needed to shape the plants or control their size. Cut the bluebeard, Russian sage, and catmint to within a few inches of the ground and the artemisias and English lavender by about half. To keep the plants shapely, prune any wayward stems of the sea buckthorn and silverberry (or the tree germander and Japanese pittosporum), and trim the lavender cotton whenever it exceeds its boundaries. The white campion is a biennial or short-lived perennial but reseeds easily; keep young plants coming along as replacements. Divide and replant the lamb's-ears and snow-in-summer after several years or whenever they begin to thin out and appear untidy.

VARIATIONS

You can turn this into a smaller rectangular planting by extending the straight edge of the top arm of the garden. Planting the smaller arm cuts the total number of blue fescue (N) to five, blue oat grass (O) to two, lavender cotton (K) to seven, globe thistle (I) to two, English lavender (H) to five, Russian sage (G) to two, and rue (F) to one.

GRAY GARDEN PLANTING PLAN

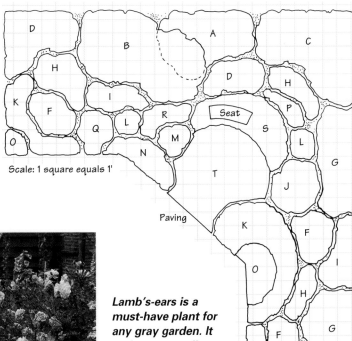

Scale: 1 square equals 1'

Paving

Lamb's-ears is a must-have plant for any gray garden. It makes an excellent edging plant and combines well with pink roses and the gray-green foliage of lavender cotton. Lamb's-ears may need replanting every few years.

THEME AND PERIOD GARDENS

For centuries, gardens have reflected the changing needs of the people who created them. The earliest gardens were practical in nature, providing their makers with food and medicine to help them survive. As populations grew more mobile, plants from different parts of the globe were exchanged and developed, and gardens became more diverse. But it wasn't until the Victorian era that gardening as we know it really hit its stride. During this period, ornamental gardening blossomed and many new design concepts were introduced.

In this chapter, you'll discover a world of outstanding garden plans, from old-world apothecary and kitchen gardens to more modern concepts such as hummingbird and butterfly gardens.

The origins of many of today's garden designs are rooted in history. Victorian gardeners, for example, are credited with the concept of creating borders using massed plantings of annuals. In this garden, 'Indian Summer' black-eyed Susan and 'Purple Wave' and 'Pink Wave' petunias are living reminders of the Victorians' influence.

AN ENGLISH COTTAGE GARDEN

A romantic rose-covered arbor is the crowning glory of a traditional English cottage garden. Tie roses to the arbor as they grow.

To suggest a design for a cottage garden is something of a contradiction. Originally, cottage gardens arose not from plans or preconceived notions but haphazardly, according to the needs and desires of the gardener and the plants available. A typical example contained an apparently random assortment of ornamentals and edibles—a mix of shrubs, perennials, and annuals. The original cottage garden was a colorful assortment of plants presented in a homey disarray—sometimes with clear pathways, sometimes without.

This plan captures the essence of a cottage garden but organizes the plants along both sides of a pathway—a scheme that could be used easily in any rectangular yard. The path need not be straight, but the surface should be as natural-looking as possible. Gravel, decomposed granite, crazy paving with spaces for thyme between the stones, and ground bark are good choices. Flowering in this garden starts in spring and continues into fall, reaching a peak in late spring to midsummer.

You can re-create this cottage garden in Zones 5 through 8 in any space that receives full sun. The list of alternative plants suggests substitutes for Zone 9 that also will extend into dry-summer Zone 10. Be sure you give the planting routine garden watering.

The happy hodgepodge that is a cottage garden needs considerable maintenance just before the growing season. Clean up dead perennial leaves and stems from last year's growth; divide and replant any perennials that are overcrowded, except for the iris, which you should reset in summer. Replace any short-lived perennials that show signs of decline. Cut back the bluebeard to within several inches of the ground. When the soil warms, set out the cosmos and sow love-in-a-mist seeds in the garden. The flowering shrubs—roses and spirea—bloom in spring; avoid pruning them back while they are dormant as this will remove potential blossoms. While they are dormant, prune only to remove dead and old, unproductive wood. Throughout the flowering season, remove the spent blooms whenever they become unsightly. After the shrubs have finished blooming, you can prune them to control their size.

ENGLISH COTTAGE GARDEN PLANTING PLAN

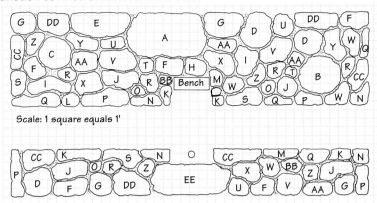

Scale: 1 square equals 1'

A cottage garden in full bloom should look natural and unplanned. The effect could be called choreographed chaos.

VARIATIONS

Although the charm of a cottage garden is fully appreciated only when you can stroll amid the plants, you can use either the wide or the narrow portion of this plan as an individual border. You may lose a little of the cottage mood, but at least you will retain the friendly jumble of plants. If you choose to plant only the narrow border, you may prefer to install a bench instead of the sundial.

ENGLISH COTTAGE GARDEN PLANTS

A–2–'Alba Maxima rose
B–1–Father Hugo's Rose (Rosa hugonis)
C–1–Spirea (Spiraea thunbergii)
D–3–Peony (Paeonia lactiflora, pink cultivar, such as 'Mons. Jules Elie')
E–2–Bluebeard (Caryopteris × clandonensis)
F–2–English lavender (Lavandula angustifolia)
G–5–Russian sage (Perovskia atriplicifolia)
H–1–Cinquefoil (Potentilla 'Katherine Dykes')
I–8–Blazing star (Liatris spicata 'Kobold')
J–22–Shasta daisy (Leucanthemum × superbum 'Polaris')
K–14–Cottage pink (Dianthus plumarius, any cultivar)
L–3–Sweet iris (Iris pallida 'Variegata')
M–5–Evergreen candytuft (Iberis sempervirens)
N–7–Snow-in-summer (Cerastium tomentosum)
O–3–Lemon daylily (Hemerocallis lilioasphodelus)
P–11–Catmint (Nepeta × faassenii)
Q–15–Lamb's-ears (Stachys byzantina)
R–11–Carolina phlox (Phlox maculata 'Miss Lingard')
S–8–Cranesbill (Geranium endressii 'Wargrave Pink')
T–4–Regal lily (Lilium regale)
U–10–Hollyhock (Alcea rosea)
V–5–Baby's breath (Gypsophila paniculata 'Bristol Fairy')
W–20–Crown pink (Lychnis coronaria)
X–11–Frikart's aster (Aster frikartii)
Y–5–New York aster (Aster novi-belgii, pink or red cultivar)
Z–8–Peachleaf bellflower (Campanula persicifolia)
AA–19–Cosmos (Cosmos bipinnatus)
BB–8–Love-in-a-mist (Nigella damascena)
CC–10–Lady's mantle (Alchemilla mollis)
DD–17–Fern-leaf yarrow (Achillea filipendulina 'Gold Plate' or 'Coronation Gold')
EE–2–'Complicata' Gallica rose

ALTERNATIVE SELECTIONS
C–1–Sun rose (Helianthemum 'Wisely Pink')
D–3–Four-o-clock (Mirabilis jalapa)
E–2–Mexican bush sage (Salvia leucantha)
H–1–Golden marguerite (Anthemis tinctoria)
I–8–Red Jupiter's beard (Centranthus ruber)
R–11–White lily-of-the-Nile (Agapanthus africanus 'Albus')
V–3–Ox-eye daisy (Leucanthemum vulgare)
CC–8–Threadleaf coreopsis (Coreopsis verticillata 'Moonbeam')

A JAPANESE GARDEN

A well-designed Japanese garden reflects the natural world around it.

The Japanese garden is a highly evolved art form that aims to capture the essence of nature's landscapes in the confines of a garden. Success is a question of choosing particular plants, carefully training and pruning them, and using certain elements as surrogates for portions of the natural landscape— for example, rocks to represent mountains or hills.

The more fortunately sited Japanese gardens borrow scenic elements from beyond the garden, such as a hillside or mountain, as backdrops to increase the illusion of space and distance. Others turn inward, becoming jewel-like microcosms within their boundaries. This Japanese scheme is of the latter, self-contained sort, with boundary fencing (perhaps of weathered wood) on three sides. It would work well as a patio garden with a paved surface leading up to the front edges.

Certain plants are inseparably associated with Japanese gardens: azaleas, bamboos, pines, and Japanese maples, to name a few. Unfortunately, a number of these key plants are broad-leaved evergreens that are impossible to grow in Zones 3 to 7. The main plant list for this garden will work in Zones 6 through 8, except for the dwarf heavenly bamboo, which is not reliably hardy in Zone 6. For these colder zones, there is no low-growing bamboolike substitute, so plant the alternative selection—Japanese barberry, which at least provides a fine texture. In Zones 9 and 10, where cold tolerance is not an issue, plant the dwarf heavenly bamboo. The plants for this garden need good light but not necessarily full sun for the entire day; four to six hours of sun will suffice.

A Japanese garden needs ongoing maintenance but nothing major at any one time. Just before the growing season starts,

JAPANESE GARDEN PLANTING PLAN

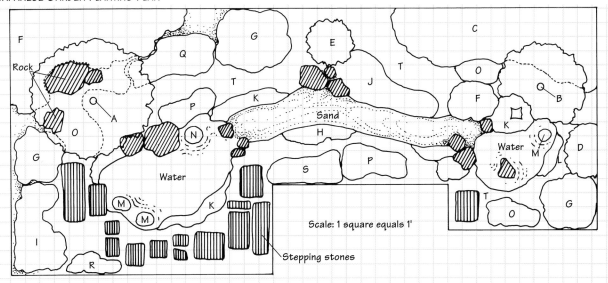

Scale: 1 square equals 1'

clean up the dead growth of the previous year. Trim ground-cover plants—the junipers and pachysandra, or alternative sweet box— if they are expanding beyond their limits; head back the dwarf heavenly bamboo and cotoneaster if you need to control their height or spread. Prune or shape the flowering shrubs—azalea and rhododendron, or Indian hawthorn—just after flowering finishes. During the growing season, remove wayward growth on plants that are overrunning their allotted spaces or departing from the shapes you intend. Keeping your garden well-manicured is an essential part of maintaining the Japanese garden look.

VARIATIONS

Because a garden in the Japanese style is conceived as an individual scene, it can't be altered in size without losing essential parts; therefore, smaller or larger gardens require different designs. You can, however, simplify this scheme by changing the pool to a raked sand bed; if you do this, the water plant, the variegated sweet flag (M) can be omitted.

JAPANESE GARDEN PLANTS

A–1–Star magnolia (Magnolia stellata)
B–1–Japanese maple (Acer palmatum)
C–3–Cranberry cotoneaster (Cotoneaster apiculatus)
D–1–Seagreen juniper (Juniperus media 'Mint Julep')
E–1–Mugo pine (Pinus mugo var. mugo)
F–6–Azalea (Rhododendron schlippenbachii)
G–3–Yaku rhododendron (Rhododendron yakushimanum)
H–3–Dwarf heavenly bamboo (Nandina domestica 'Harbor Dwarf')
I–2–Juniper (Juniperus sabina 'Blue Danube')
J–2–Creeping juniper (Juniperus horizontalis 'Wiltonii')
K–29–Creeping lilyturf (Liriope spicata)
L–4–Hosta (Hosta sieboldiana or H. glauca)
M–3–Variegated sweet flag (Acorus gramineus 'Variegatus')
N–1–Yellow flag iris (Iris pseudacorus)
O–20–Pachysandra (Pachysandra terminalis)
P–9–Japanese blood grass (Imperata cylindrica 'Rubra' or 'Red Baron')
Q–8–Japanese anemone (Anemone hybrida 'Honorine Jobert')
R–10–Leather bergenia (Bergenia crassifolia)
S–10–Ajuga (Ajuga reptans)
T–Irish moss (Sagina subulata) (several flats: 2-inch squares cut and planted 6 inches apart)

ALTERNATIVE SELECTIONS
F–6–Azalea (Rhododendron, Kurume hybrid, such as 'Hinodegiri' or 'Hino-Crimson')
G–3–Indian hawthorn (Rhaphiolepis indica 'Ballerina')
H–3–Japanese barberry (Berberis thunbergii 'Crimson Pygmy' for Zones 6 and 7)
K–29–Mondo grass (Ophiopogon japonicus)
L–4–Lenten rose (Helleborus orientalis)
O–8–Dwarf sweet box (Sarcococca hookeriana var. humilis)

Water is an essential element of a Japanese garden. Stone lanterns add an Asian influence.

A VICTORIAN CARPET-BEDDING GARDEN

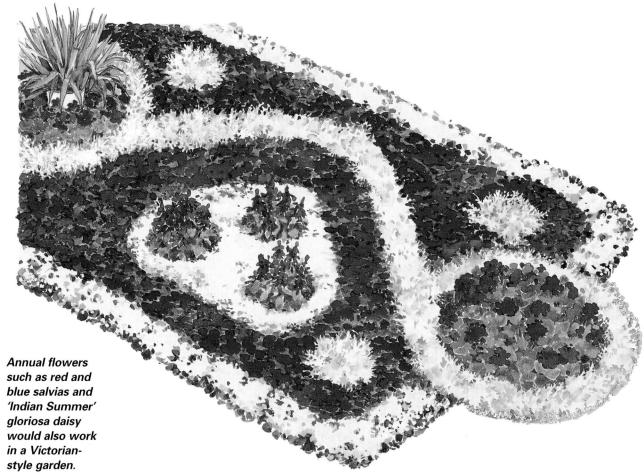

Annual flowers such as red and blue salvias and 'Indian Summer' gloriosa daisy would also work in a Victorian-style garden.

The Victorian penchant for elaborate ornamentation extended even into the garden. Borrowing from the older traditions of parterres and knot gardens, and working with an assortment of colorful annuals, Victorian gardeners developed a planting style that evoked the richness and intricacy of Persian carpets—hence the term carpet bedding. Think of this garden as a type of knot garden (see pages 46 and 47) untied. In place of rigidly controlled lines and curves within a square frame, carpet-bedding design introduced flowing curves, loops, and even heraldic-style decorative motifs executed in low-growing flowering and foliage plants.

Many of the most impressive Victorian examples of carpet bedding were designed on a grand scale: circles, ovals, or squares set in lawns of estates and parks; and long curving or rectangular beds bordering public and private drives. A typical bedding scheme employed a repeated design and often featured an exotic centerpiece such as a palm or yucca.

This bedding plan incorporates both of these concepts. The garden is small but expandable and reasonably simple to lay out,

VICTORIAN CARPET-BEDDING PLANTING PLAN   Scale: 1 square equals 1'

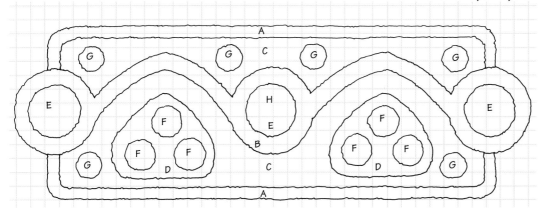

especially if you mark the design on bare earth with a sprinkling of flour or gypsum.

Plant this garden where it will receive sun all day. A surrounding lawn nicely sets off the colorful floral tapestry, as does a gravel path around the garden. Also, water and deadhead regularly because the garden's effectiveness depends on it being continually in bloom.

Because this colorful carpet is made from annuals and plants treated as annuals, it is suitable for all zones. The alternative list provides a different color scheme featuring yellow, white, and blue. You will need to replant the annuals each spring, but you can keep the potted accent plant year after year. Choose one adapted to your zone, or move a tender specimen indoors for the winter.

Each spring you need to start maintenance literally from the ground up. Remove last year's spent plants, rework the soil, lay out the design, or a new design of your choosing, then set out new plants when the soil has warmed. During the growing season, the garden will need grooming.

VARIATIONS

You can lengthen the bed by adding additional circles and connecting "ribbons" within the bed, repeating the design. With a little planning, you can even bend or curve the extended planting into a crescent shape. You could also vary the design by choosing plants with different flower colors. Many annuals are available in different colors. Salvia, for example, comes in red, blue, purple, cream, and white.

VICTORIAN CARPET-BEDDING PLANTS

A—96—Wax begonia (*Begonia semperflorens-cultorum*, red-foliaged selection)
B—64—Dusty miller (*Tanacetum ptarmiciflorum* 'Silver Feather' or *Senecio cineraria* 'Cirrus')
C—115—Garden verbena (*Verbena hybrida*, red selection)
D—56—Sweet alyssum (*Lobularia maritima*, white selection)
E—15—Common geranium (*Pelargonium × hortorum*, red selection)
F—30—Scarlet sage (*Salvia splendens*, red selection)
G—18—Dusty miller (*Senecio cineraria* 'Silver Dust')
H—1—Accent plant in pot, such as grass palm (*Cordyline australis*), sago palm (*Cycas revoluta*), New Zealand flax (*Phormium tenax*), bird-of-paradise (*Strelitzia reginae*), or Adam's needle (*Yucca filamentosa* or *Y. flaccida*)

ALTERNATIVE SELECTIONS
A—96—French marigold (*Tagetes patula*, yellow selection)
B—90—Wax begonia (*Begonia semperflorens-cultorum*, white selection)
C—115—Petunia (*Petunia hybrida*, blue selection)
E—15—Common geranium (*Pelargonium × hortorum*, white selection)
F—30—Marigold (*Tagetes spp.*, yellow-flowered hybrid)

The key to a successful carpet-bedding garden is to pair complementary colors. For example, this scarlet sage and violet ageratum create a vibrant color scheme all summer long.

A KNOT GARDEN

From purely utilitarian beginnings in medieval times, gardening in Western Europe took an increasingly decorative tack during the Renaissance. A penchant for clipped hedging and topiary work culminated in elaborate parterres. The knot garden—a square garden containing a geometric, ribbonlike interweaving of dwarf clipped hedges around accent plants—was developed in the 16th and 17th centuries. In each knot, the spaces between the ribbons were filled with herbs, flowers, or colored pebbles. A basic knot garden contained four such knots, separated by pathways. A later tradition used boxwood (*Buxus sempervirens*) exclusively. This change retained the essential geometry of the style but lost the woven appearance of different foliages. Myrtle and wall germander are two other good hedging alternatives.

Many knot patterns contained arcs, circles, and elaborate curlicues. The pattern presented here uses straight lines, designed for simple execution. The plants on the main list are a traditional mix of herbs, all of which will grow in Zones 5 through 9 and dry-summer Zone 10. For a more colorful knot, consider the alternative selections, which thrive in the same zones. The alternative plants also fall in the herb category, though the pot marigolds are also often grown as bedding annuals.

An attractive knot garden depends on crisp edges, and this means frequent trimming. During the growing season, give the hedges a light shearing every week or two. Periodically trim the herbs to keep them

Herbs with colorful foliage, such as these variegated sages, work well in knot gardens. Other possible herbs include lavender cotton, germander, thyme, and myrtle.

KNOT GARDEN PLANTS

A–84–Wall germander (*Teucrium chamaedrys*)
B–40–Lavender cotton (*Santolina chamaecyparissus*)
C–40–Green lavender cotton (*Santolina virens*)
D–12–Tricolor garden sage (*Salvia officinalis* 'Tricolor')
E–12–Variegated garden sage (*Salvia officinalis* 'Icterina')
F–12–Hyssop (*Hyssopus officinalis*)
G–12–Sweet marjoram (*Origanum majorana*)
H–4–English lavender (*Lavandula angustifolia* 'Munstead')
I–Gravel or crushed rocks

ALTERNATIVE SELECTIONS
D–12–Lemon thyme (*Thymus × citriodorus*)
E–12–Silver thyme (*Thymus vulgaris* 'Argenteus')
F–24–Pot marigold (*Calendula officinalis*, dwarf cream selection)
G–24–Pot marigold (*Calendula officinalis*, dwarf yellow selection)

KNOT GARDEN PLANTING PLAN

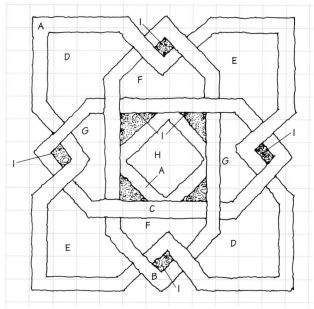

Scale: 1 square equals 1'

within their assigned boundaries and to maintain somewhat uniform surfaces. Plants on both lists need full sun. The plants on the main list are perennials or small shrubs, all of which will live for a number of years with only moderate watering (they can take some dryness between waterings). Especially where summer rainfall is the rule, make sure the soil is well-drained. Among the alternative plants, the pot marigolds must be planted anew each year.

VARIATIONS

As long as you retain the concept of precise interlacing ribbons of plants, you can work countless variations on a knot garden by changing the plants. For the hedge, choose plants that will not grow big, that have small, dense leaves, and can be closely clipped.

There are numerous possibilities for the hedges. You could use boxwood interwoven with Japanese barberry (*Berberis thunbergii* 'Crimson Pygmy'). In the cool-summer regions of Zones 7, 8, and 9, you could interweave hedges of heaths (*Erica*) or heathers (*Calluna*) in contrasting foliage colors. Choices for the spaces between the ribbons are truly far-ranging. Imagine a knot garden planted with a single sweep of dwarf marigolds, zinnias, salvia, petunias, or even dwarf sunflowers.

The space between the knots can be filled with anything. Traditionally, a mulch or colored gravel was used to create a carpet pattern.

A ROCK GARDEN

Hen and chicks are ideal for rock gardens. They are almost maintenance-free and thrive in hot, dry conditions. Young chicks are easy to divide and use elsewhere.

In its most sophisticated form, a rock garden re-creates the rock-strewn landscape found above the timberline on a mountain. It is a garden for choice, culturally demanding alpine plants. At its other most casual extreme, the rock garden may be a dry-set stone retaining wall embellished with prostrate annuals, perennials, and succulents that find rootholds in the crevices. Many rock-gardening enthusiasts practice an art that lies somewhere between the two extremes, designing gardens that skillfully mingle rocks and small plants in a naturalistic manner.

This rock-garden plan features easy-to-grow shrubs and perennials, all of which are good rock-garden subjects because of their sizes and growth habits. Plants in the main list will thrive in a sunny location in Zones 5 through 8 where summers are humid and in Zones 5 through 9 where summers are fairly dry. Gardeners in dry-summer Zone 10 should substitute plants from the alternative selections; gardeners in dry-summer Zone 9 may use plants from either list. In all zones, give the plants well-drained soil and regular watering. Although the rock-garden plan is shown as a ground-level garden surrounded by pathways, you might want to use the same plan for a raised garden or even for a planting on a gentle slope.

Because you won't be able to find rocks that exactly match the sizes or configurations indicated, consider the plan a general guide rather than a blueprint. Use it as a key to harmonious plant associations and as an illustration of natural-appearing rock groupings.

When selecting rocks, choose those native to your area, if possible. Local rocks will look the most natural. Set rocks as they would appear in nature. A garden of craggy miniature Matterhorns, for example, look artificial.

Maintaining a rock garden is an ongoing exercise in tidying. There is never a great amount of labor at one time, but neglected edges show up clearly. Begin by removing dead leaves and old flowering stems in late winter or early spring, then assess the condition of the plants. Lightly head back or shear spreading shrubs and perennials overgrowing their bounds. Replace any shorter-lived perennials (such as evergreen candytuft) that remained sparse or patchy after last year's trimming. During the growing season, remove spent flowers as they fade.

VARIATIONS

Remembering that this planting scheme is a general guide rather than a blueprint, you can

ROCK GARDEN PLANTING PLAN

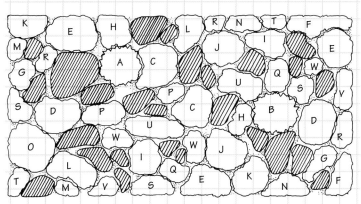

Scale: 1 square equals 1'

vary the garden's dimensions and size to suit your space and assortment of rocks. All the plants except the conifers and shrubs are low-growing, with the very lowest-profile individuals at the perimeter of the garden. If you alter the size of the plan, use the perimeter plants to finish off the edges.

ROCK GARDEN PLANTS

A–1–Dwarf Hinoki false cypress (*Chamaecyparis obtusa* 'Nana')
B–1–Oriental arborvitae (*Platycladus orientalis* 'Minima Glauca')
C–2–Heath (*Erica carnea*) or Heather (*Calluna vulgaris*)
D–2–Japanese barberry (*Berberis thunbergii* 'Crimson Pygmy')
E–3–Sun rose (*Helianthemum nummularium*)
F–5–Woolly thyme (*Thymus pseudolanuginosus*)
G–6–Hen and chicks (*Sempervivum tectorum*)
H–3–Ozark Sundrops (*Oenothera missourensis*)
I–2–Moss pink (*Phlox subulata*)
J–4–Evergreen candytuft (*Iberis sempervirens*)
K–5–Wall rockcress (*Arabis caucasica*)
L–3–Basket-of-gold (*Aurinia saxatilis*)
M–4–Dianthus 'Tiny Rubies'
N–5–Dianthus 'Bath's Pink'
O–1–Soapwort (*Saponaria officinalis*)
P–3–Japanese blood grass (*Imperata cylindrica* 'Rubra')
Q–4–Woolly yarrow (*Achillea tomentosa*)
R–5–Sea thrift (*Armeria maritima*)
S–6–Cranesbill (*Geranium cinereum*)
T–5–Sedum (*Sedum spathulifolium*)
U–4–Cranesbill (*Geranium endressii* 'Wargrave Pink')
V–5–Cinquefoil (*Potentilla cinerea*)
W–5–Cottage pink (*Dianthus plumarius*)

ALTERNATIVE SELECTIONS
A–1–Japanese cedar (*Cryptomeria japonica* 'Lobbii' or ' Nana')
C–2–Dwarf jasmine (*Jasminum parkeri*)
D–2–Heavenly bamboo (*Nandina domestica* 'Nana')
I–2–Fan flower (*Scaevola* 'Blue Fans')
V–5–English daisy (*Bellis perennis*)

Take advantage of the planting pockets between the stones when planting a rock garden. Pack soil into these pockets and tuck in small perennial and annual flowers.

A DESERT GARDEN

When you're creating a garden in a hostile climate such as the desert, you want to focus on plants that are native to the area. Native prickly pear cactus, for example, stands up to heat and drought and produces spectacular flowers in springtime.

Mention the word desert and the images that come to mind no doubt contain sand, rocks, cacti, and sagebrush. This desert garden offers those classic elements along with some Southwestern standbys—yucca, agave, and an assortment of colorful wildflowers.

Aridity is only one desert characteristic. A desert that contains all the classic elements mentioned above will have fairly mild winter temperatures: Most cacti and succulents are unable to survive temperatures many degrees below freezing. Even though this desert planting scheme contains some of the most cold-tolerant of those plants, it will succeed only in dry-summer parts of Zones 8, 9, and 10. Gardeners in the dry-summer areas of Zones 9 and 10 can choose from the alternative selections as well. (In fact, Zone 10 gardeners can choose freely from any well-stocked cactus and succulent nursery.) The sagebrush in the main list may, in time, outgrow its space. If you don't want to bother with occasional restrictive pruning, choose the saltbush on the alternative list (though at the expense of the sagebrush aroma).

Naturally a desert garden needs full sun, and just as naturally it doesn't need frequent watering. Give these plants well-drained soil and apply water judiciously. Water all plants immediately after planting, then let the cacti

establish new roots (a four- to eight-week process) before watering them again. The plants need water in spring, summer, and early fall; water thoroughly, then let the soil dry before watering again. In the dormant period, brought on by the shortening of days and cooler weather in fall and winter, water only if garden plants show signs of stress, such as shriveling or drooping.

A desert planting requires minimal maintenance, the occasional work focusing simply on neatness. In late winter, remove spent stems from the evening primroses and California fuchsia; clear the garden of dead leaves and tidy up the plants. If necessary, prune the sagebrush or saltbush to control its size.

VARIATIONS

You can shorten this desert garden to 18 feet by drawing a line between the two points indicated on the plan, then planting only the larger portion. This leaves you with all the desert essence except the tall fishhook barrel cactus.

DESERT GARDEN PLANTING PLAN   Scale: 1 square equals 1'

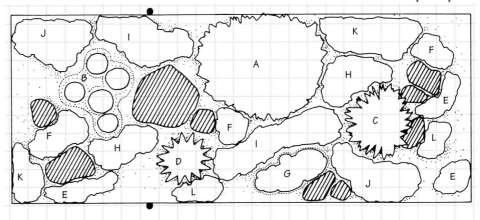

DESERT GARDEN PLANTS

A–1–Big sagebrush (Artemisia tridentata)
B–5–Fishhook barrel cactus (Ferocactus wislizeni)
C–1–Small soapweed (Yucca glauca)
D–1–Utah agave (Agave utahensis)
E–13–Hen and chicks (Sempervivum tectorum)
F–8–Purple fountain grass (Pennisetum setaceum 'Cupreum')
G–2–Beavertail (Opuntia basilaris) or other prickly pear cactus
H–8–Mexican evening primrose (Oenothera berlandieri)
I–10–Baja evening primrose (Oenothera stubbei or O. drummondii)
J–20–Ice plant (Delosperma cooperi)
K–9–California fuchsia (Zauschneria californica var. latifolia or
    Z. septentrionalis)
L–4–Sulfurflower (Eriogonum umbellatum)

ALTERNATIVE SELECTIONS
A–1–Fourwing saltbush (Atriplex canescens)
B–2–Organpipe cactus (Lemaireocereus thurberi)
C–1–Adam's needle (Yucca filamentosa)
E–13–Hen and chicks (Echeveria hybrids)
G–2–Hedgehog cactus (Echinocereus engelmannii)

To keep your desert garden colorful consider adding a few annual flowers that are naturally heat- and drought-tolerant. Marigolds, for example, won't wilt when the mercury soars.

AN APOTHECARY GARDEN

Before the days of drug stores and prescription medicines, gardens such as this one provided natural remedies for illness and disease.

During the Middle Ages in Western Europe, the preservation and spread of knowledge were the province of the church. Included in this knowledge was the practice of medicine, and no respectable monastery would be without its apothecary garden of plants to be administered as remedies or preventives.

This planting scheme offers an attractive assortment of medieval medicinal plants. For easy access, a path separates the planting into two beds that face a central sundial to remind the attending monk both of the time of day and of the eternalness of time itself. Note the number of plants that bear the epithet "officinalis," a Latin word meaning "of the workshop," which was later applied to the plants that were standard components of medieval pharmacies.

All the plants on the main list will thrive in Zones 5 through 9 and dry-summer Zone 10. The alternative selections offer foliage variations for the same zones. By choosing any or all of the alternative plants, you can vary the color scheme in the garden.

Late winter or early spring is the time to clean out the previous year's dead foliage and spent stems and to prune the shrubs. Lightly prune the rose if the plant has become rangy. Cut back the southernwood to within a few inches of the ground, and cut back the English lavender by about half. Trim rue and garden sage as needed to keep these plants compact. In time, some of the perennials will

APOTHECARY GARDEN PLANTING PLAN

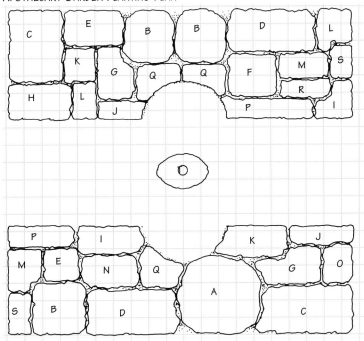

Scale: 1 square equals 1'

Surprisingly, many common garden plants were used in apothecary gardens. Early herbalists used plants to cure everything from stomach pains to fever. Animals, too, were treated with herbal remedies.

start to spread beyond their allotted spaces. When this happens, simply remove a few plants. If a perennial becomes sparse or patchy, dig it up and divide and replant it in late winter or early spring. When the iris become crowded (in four or five years), dig them up and divide after they bloom. Although the planting contains drought-tolerant plants and also two mints that are rampant in moist soil, routine garden watering suits them all. Place the beds where they'll receive sun for more than half the day.

VARIATIONS

By planting either one of the two beds, you will have a varied garden of apothecary plants that fits into a smaller space. To finish off either bed as a complete rectangle, plant pot marigolds (T) in the semicircular inset along the front edge and include the sundial if you wish. If you're short on garden space, grow your favorite medicinal plants in containers. Mint, thyme, lavender, sage, pot marigold, horehound, lemon balm, violet, and roses make terrific pot plants. Place the containers in a sunny location and water whenever the soil feels dry to the touch. Tall varieties such as common fennel, southernwood, lovage, and comfrey do not make good container plants.

APOTHECARY GARDEN PLANTS

A–1–Apothecary rose (Rosa gallica 'Officinalis')
B–3–Rue (Ruta graveolens)
C–6–Valerian (Valeriana officinalis)
D–4–English lavender (Lavandula angustifolia)
E–3–Common fennel (Foeniculum vulgare)
F–1–Lovage (Levisticum officinale)
G–4–Garden sage (Salvia officinalis)
H–2–Southernwood (Artemisia abrotanum)
I–6–Orris root (Iris germanica var. florentina)
J–7–Sweet violet (Viola odorata)
K–5–Horehound (Marrubium vulgare)
L–4–Lemon balm (Melissa officinalis)
M–6–Costmary (Tanacetum balsamita)
N–2–Comfrey (Symphytum officinale)
O–4–Sweet marjoram (Origanum majorana)
P–7–Common thyme (Thymus vulgaris)
Q–6–Betony (Stachys officinalis)
R–2–Spearmint (Mentha spicata)
S–4–Peppermint (Mentha × piperita)
T–8–Pot marigold (Calendula officinalis) around sundial

ALTERNATIVE SELECTIONS
B–3–Variegated rue (Ruta graveolens 'Variegata')
E–3–Bronze fennel (Foeniculum vulgare purpureum)
G–4–Tricolor garden sage (Salvia officinalis 'Tricolor'), variegated garden sage (S. officinalis 'Icterina'), or purple garden sage (S. officinalis 'Purpurascens')
L–4–Variegated lemon balm (Melissa officinalis 'Aurea')
P–7–Silver thyme (Thymus vulgaris 'Argenteus')
T–8–Pot marigold (Calendula officinalis, yellow or cream selection)

A DEVOTIONAL GARDEN

For some gardeners, a devotional garden is a place that re-creates a garden mentioned in the Bible. Others may find it an escape from the everyday world, a place of reflection and peace.

Although the Bible mentions numerous plants, many of them need the relatively mild winter of the Holy Land in order to survive—and today quite a few would be looked upon as weeds. To create an attractive planting with religious associations that will grow in Zones 5 through 10, it was necessary to turn to the colder climate of Western Europe and draw upon a variety of medieval devotional sources. Ideas for this garden were gleaned from the great number of 15th century artworks, tapestries, poems, carols and hymns, religious texts, and seasonal rituals associated with the Virgin Mary and the Christ Child. The alternative selections are additional choices for the same zones. The planting scheme was designed to accommodate a statue such as the Madonna and Child shown here.

Establish this bed where it will receive sun for more than half the day; give the plants routine garden watering. In late winter or early spring, clean out the dead leaves and spent flowering stems from the previous year's growth. To keep the roses shapely, lightly head them back if they need it. Replant the three annuals—pot marigold, bachelor's button, and Shirley poppy. If you choose

the Johnny-jump-up instead of the English daisy, set out new plants—or transplant the self-sown seedlings—each year. Every other year replace the biennial dames rocket and hollyhock. Both of these plants frequently self-sow, so young plants can be dug and transplanted to other areas of the garden.

VARIATIONS

To make a shorter bed with the statue at the center of the front edge, draw a curved line between the two points indicated on the planting plan, which mimics the curve at the right edge of the plan. You will lose one planting of lady's mantle (C) and all of the English daisy (K), bachelor's button (O), and pot marigold (N).

DEVOTIONAL GARDEN PLANTS

A–1–'Semiplena' rose
B–1–Apothecary rose (Rosa gallica 'Officinalis')
C–10–Lady's mantle (Alchemilla mollis)
D–4–Lily-of-the-valley (Convallaria majalis)
E–4–Carnation (Dianthus caryophyllus)
F–2–Bearded iris (Iris germanica)
G–4–European columbine (Aquilegia vulgaris)
H–5–Rose campion (Lychnis coronaria)
I–5–Madonna lily (Lilium candidum)
J–6–Hollyhock (Alcea rosea)
K–4–English daisy (Bellis perennis)
L–10–Sweet violet (Viola odorata)
M–6–Dames rocket (Hesperis matronalis)
N–9–Pot marigold (Calendula officinalis)
O–7–Bachelor's button (Centaurea cyanus)
P–8–Shirley poppy
    (Papaver rhoeas)

ALTERNATIVE SELECTIONS
D–3–Spearmint (Mentha
    spicata)
K–4–Johnny-jump-up (Viola
    tricolor)
L–6–Common periwinkle
    (Vinca minor)

Towering hollyhocks are a must-have plant for any devotional garden. Thought to have been brought back from the Holy Land to England by the Crusaders, the flowers took their name from a combination of "holly" (Middle English for holy) and "hock" meaning a member of the mallow family.

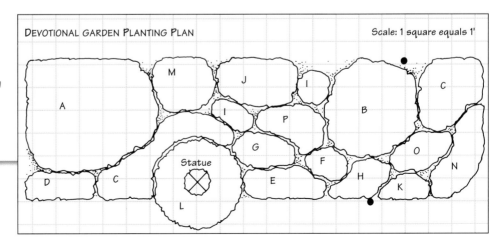

DEVOTIONAL GARDEN PLANTING PLAN   Scale: 1 square equals 1'

A SHAKESPEARE GARDEN

Espalier, the art of training trees against a wall or other support to expose fruit to the sun, was popular in Shakespeare's day. Gardens were often enclosed by a "fence" of interwoven espaliered apple or pear trees—a good way to grow lots of fruit in a small space.

From Titania's bower in *A Midsummer Night's Dream* to Perdita's rustic garden in *The Winter's Tale*, Shakespeare's writings abound with references to plants and gardens. What a simple pleasure, then, to establish a quiet garden enclave with plants that recall the Bard.

Most of Shakespeare's plants that we would consider gardenworthy won't survive winters in Zones 3, 4, and 5; quite a few can't even take the low temperatures in Zone 6. The planting suggested here contains some of the most adaptable of his plants, suitable for many zones. All the plants on the main list will grow in Zones 6 through 9, although the potted laurel will need to be taken indoors during the winter in Zones 6, 7, and 8. Gardeners in Zone 9 and dry-summer Zone 10 will want to choose the Japanese boxwood instead of the common boxwood, and one of the alternative dwarf apple trees. They may also prefer the lemon tree alternate for the potted laurel. The English daisy and iris will succeed in Zones 6 through 10.

Locate these beds where they'll receive sun for at least six hours a day. The year's maintenance starts with cleanup and pruning—either in fall or in late winter or early spring before growth begins. Clear out the dead leaves and flowering stems of the perennials, and remove the spent annuals— larkspur and pot marigold. In late winter or early spring, remove unproductive rose stems and lightly trim any wayward canes to shape

SHAKESPEARE GARDEN PLANTS

A–3– Gallica rose (Rosa gallica 'Versicolor' or 'Rosa Mundi')
B–1–Apple (Malus pumila on dwarfing rootstock)
C–1–Sweetbriar (Rosa rubiginosa)
D–1–'Semiplena' rose (Rosa alba 'semi-plena')
E–1–'Maidens Blush' rose (Rosa alba 'Maiden's Blush')
F–1–Rue (Ruta graveolens)
G–2–Common wormwood (Artemisia absinthium)
H–40–Common boxwood (Buxus sempervirens)
I–11–English lavender (Lavandula angustifolia)
J–2–Rhubarb (Rheum rhabarbarum)
K–3–Madonna lily (Lilium candidum)
L–3–Hyssop (Hyssopus officinalis)
M–4–European columbine (Aquilegia vulgaris)
N–7–Cottage pink (Dianthus plumarius)
O–9–Chamomile (Chamaemelum nobile)
P–8–Larkspur (Consolida ambigua)
Q–6–Pot marigold (Calendula officinalis)
R–1–Laurel (Laurus nobilis, in container)
S–1–Common thyme (Thymus vulgaris)
T–18–Sweet violet (Viola odorata)

ALTERNATIVE SELECTIONS

B–1–Apple (Malus pumila 'Beverly Hills', 'Ein Shemer', or 'Gordon' on dwarfing rootstock)
H–40–Japanese boxwood (Buxus microphylla var. japonica)
J–16–English daisy (Bellis perennis)
K–1–Yellow flag iris (Iris pseudacorus)
R–1–Lemon (Citrus limon) or orange (C. sinensis), in container

SHAKESPEARE GARDEN PLANTING PLAN

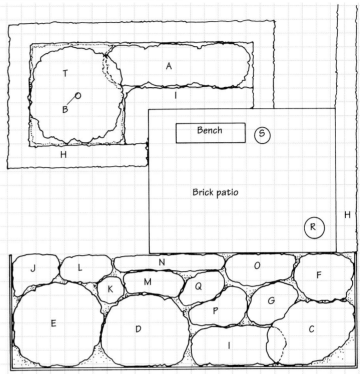

Scale: 1 square equals 1'

the plants (pruning these roses before they bloom sacrifices some of the spring flowers). Also cut the English lavender, common wormwood, and hyssop back halfway, and prune the rue as needed to keep it shapely. Set out new plants of larkspur and pot marigold. During the growing season, shear the boxwood and English lavender hedges as often as needed to suit your sense of neatness. In cold climates wait until after the weather warms up in spring and the plants begin to develop new growth to prune the lavender and boxwood. Give all plants routine garden watering and control weeds as necessary.

VARIATIONS

This scheme was designed to be a cozy nook in a corner of the garden, where you might sit and read among "literary" plants. Either bed, though, could stand on its own as an individual planting.

Shakespearean gardens display the plants mentioned in the Bard's plays, for example, "I know a bank whereon the wild thyme blows. . . ."

AN HERB GARDEN

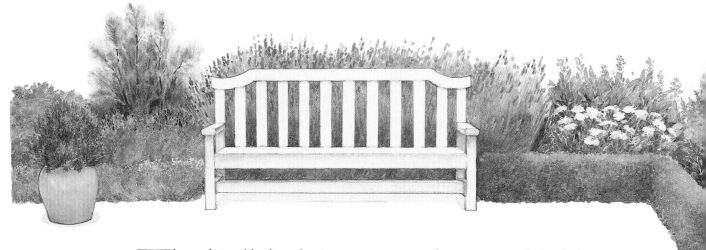

Colorful and fragrant, an herb garden is a sensual delight. Herb gardens are often centered around a focal point such as a sundial or bee skep. A location near the kitchen door makes for easy clipping.

The traditional herb garden is a romantic notion perhaps no more than one hundred years old. In it are combined curative plants of the medieval apothecary gardens, culinary herbs from the kitchen garden, and diverse other plants that blend in well. The traditional style of herb garden, fully realized in Edwardian times, emphasized the aesthetic relationship between the plants and favored those that were pleasantly aromatic so that the garden would be pleasing to eyes and nose alike. Some of these gardens were formal in design, recalling knot gardens and European parterres; others were more similar to the cottage garden style, their artfully haphazard arrangements bordered by an herbal hedge.

This herb garden incorporates both a cottage effect and a little formality and offers an enchanting cross section of herbs of all sorts. The sundial is in the Edwardian style; the bench—a timeless garden amenity—

is a place to pause and absorb the romance of it all. Although several plants boast striking flower displays (especially the English lavender, bee balm, and common yarrow), much of the beauty of this garden lies in foliage of differing colors and textures. All the plants but three will thrive in Zones 6 through 9 and dry-summer Zone 10. The potted rosemary and geranium will need to be brought indoors during the winter in Zones 6 and 7. In Zone 10, instead of bee balm choose the alternative selection, golden feverfew. The other alternative selections are presented as options to vary the planting. Give the plants full sun and moderate to routine watering. Well-drained soil is preferable; in summer-rainfall regions it is a requirement.

Trimming and tidying are the main maintenance obligations for this herb planting. In fall, late winter, or early spring, remove the dead leaves and cut out last year's

Herb gardens are most fragrant after a rain or whenever the wind blows. Harvest herbs just before they bloom for the best flavor.

HERB GARDEN PLANTS

A–3–English lavender (Lavandula angustifolia)
B–1–Rue (Ruta graveolens)
C–1–Common wormwood (Artemisia absinthium)
D–1–Bronze fennel (Foeniculum vulgare purpureum)
E–1–Southernwood (Artemisia abrotanum)
F–1–Garden sage (Salvia officinalis)
G–1–Variegated garden sage (Salvia officinalis 'Icterina')
H–1–Tricolor garden sage (Salvia officinalis 'Tricolor')
I–1–Purple garden sage (Salvia officinalis 'Purpurascens')
J–3–Common yarrow (Achillea millefolium)
K–4–Costmary (Tanacetum balsamita)
L–2–Hyssop (Hyssopus officinalis)
M–4–Silver thyme (Thymus vulgaris 'Argenteus')
N–2–Bee balm (Monarda didyma)
O–17–Wall germander (Teucrium chamaedrys)
P–2–Lavender cotton (Santolina chamaecyparissus)
Q–5–Chamomile (Chamaemelum nobile)
R–2–Oregano (Origanum vulgare)
S–3–Lamb's-ears (Stachys byzantina)
T–1–Winter savory (Satureja montana)
U–4–Chives (Allium schoenoprasum)
V–1–Rosemary, in pot (Rosmarinus officinalis)

ALTERNATIVE SELECTIONS
A–2–Apothecary's rose (R. gallica 'Officinalis')
D–1–Common tansy (Tanacetum vulgare)
K–4–Horehound (Marrubium vulgare)
N–4–Golden feverfew (Tanacetum parthenium 'Aureum')
Q–4–Lemon balm (Melissa officinalis)
S–2–Catnip (Nepeta cataria)
T–1–French sorrel (Rumex scutatus)
V–1–Apple geranium (Pelargonium odoratissimum)

flowering stems on the common yarrow, costmary, bee balm, and lamb's-ears. Then in late winter or early spring, cut back by half the English lavender, the garden sages, hyssop, and oregano. This is also an appropriate time to even up the wall germander border. Later in the year you may need to lightly clip it again to keep it neat. The bronze fennel may seed prolifically in Zones 7 through 10, so in those zones it is better to cut it back toward the end of the growing season (late summer or early fall) before its seeds ripen and scatter. Trim the silver thyme, common wormwood, southernwood, lavender cotton, and rue as needed, not always every year, to keep them from becoming rangy or sparse.

To ensure winter survival in Zone 6, protect the English lavender, lavender cotton, and winter savory with evergreen boughs or a loose covering of salt hay in late fall.

VARIATIONS

Although designed as a peaceful enclave, this planting can be reduced to two L-shaped plans, either of which can be slotted into a smaller space. To make the smaller of the two L shapes, draw a line from the back of the bed to the front, between the English lavender (A) and the fennel (D), hyssop (L), and thyme (M). Plant the portion with the lavender, eliminating the bench and continuing the wall

germander (O) border around the lavender. For a larger L-shaped bed, draw a line on the other side of the English lavender from the back of the bed to the front, and again plant the portion containing the lavender. In this option, retain the bench. You could border the front edge of this garden with wall germander (O).

HERB GARDEN PLANTING PLAN   Scale: 1 square equals 1'

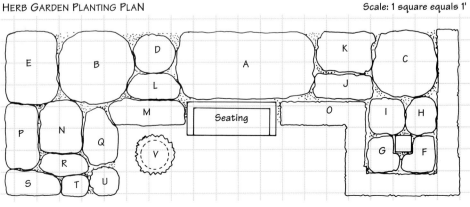

A FRAGRANT GARDEN

A garden without fragrance is like a movie without a sound track. In this border, a hedge of pink phlox perfumes the entire garden in midsummer.

Fragrance is the attribute that places many attractive flowers in the "especially beautiful" category. It also elevates more mundane plants to a special status. A pleasing aroma not only enhances the moment, but it also calls up fond memories associated with the particular scent. Few things are more soul-satisfying than having a corner of a garden devoted to olfactory as well as visual pleasure.

Flower and plant aromas are infinitely varied, and scents are dispersed in several ways. Some blossoms release their fragrance into the air, perfuming a garden from a distance. Others reveal their scent only when you put your nose into their petals. Plants with aromatic foliage may not bring their essential oils into effect until you brush against them or bruise their leaves. This garden contains representatives of all three types of fragrant plants.

From the first violets in late winter or early spring to the final roses of fall, this fragrance planting offers flowers and scent almost continually. The peak display will be in early to midsummer, when all but the violets, iris, and peony will be blooming. Give the plants at least six hours of sun each day and routine garden watering. With two exceptions, the plants in the main list will grow in Zones 5 through 9 and dry-summer Zone 10. The apple geranium (in the container) should spend winter protected from frost in Zones 5 through 9; while the peony's need for winter chilling means it won't bloom in Zones 9 and 10. The alternative list gives a peony substitute—the wallflower—for Zones 9 and 10, as well as several notably fragrant options for those two warm zones.

In mid- to late fall in Zones 5 and 6, put the 'Penelope' rose "to bed" for the winter; see Ortho's *All About Roses* for recommended methods of protecting roses.

FRAGRANT GARDEN PLANTING PLAN

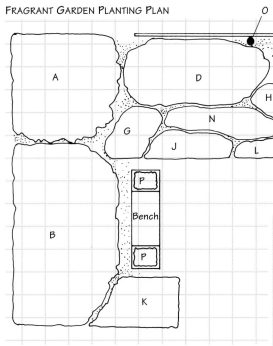

Scale: 1 square equals 1'

FRAGRANT GARDEN PLANTS

A–1–Common butterfly bush (*Buddleia davidii*)
B–2–'Penelope' rose
C–1–'Frau Dagmar Hartopp' rose
D–2–English lavender (*Lavandula angustifolia*)
E–1–Peony (*Paeonia lactiflora* 'Mons. Jules Elie')
F–1–Southernwood (*Artemisia abrotanum*)
G–2–Bearded iris 'Victoria Falls'
H–2–Madonna lily (*Lilium candidum*)
I–7–Cottage pink (*Dianthus plumarius*)
J–5–Cheddar pink (*Dianthus gratianopolitanus*)
K–8–Sweet violet (*Viola odorata*)
L–5–Mignonette (*Reseda odorata*)
M–12–Sweet alyssum (*Lobularia maritima*)
N–8–Flowering tobacco (*Nicotiana alata*)
O–1–Woodbine (*Lonicera periclymenum* 'Serotina')
P–2–Apple geranium, in container (*Pelargonium odoratissimum*)

ALTERNATIVE SELECTIONS
A–1–Sweet olive (*Osmanthus fragrans*)
E–2–Wallflower (*Erysimum linifolium* 'Variegatum')
O–1–Star jasmine (*Trachelospermum jasminoides*)
P–2–Gardenia, in container (*Gardenia agusta* 'Veitchii')

In all zones, yearly maintenance starts in late winter or early spring with cleanup and pruning. Clear out dead leaves, spent flower stems, and remains of last year's annuals: flowering tobacco, mignonette, and sweet alyssum. Remove winter protection from the 'Penelope' rose if necessary, then prune all of the roses to shape them. Cut the English lavender and southernwood back halfway, and the butterfly bush to 6 to 12 inches from the ground.

Replant the sweet alyssum and mignonette when you can work the soil; set out new flowering tobacco plants when the soil has warmed. Replace plantings of cheddar pink, cottage pink, and wallflower with cuttings or new plants when existing plantings become sparse and rangy. Dig and divide the bearded iris every third or fourth summer. If the bearded iris become too crowded, they will produce fewer flowers.

VARIATIONS

You can alter the shape of this planting (though you'll sacrifice a place to rest and savor the scents) by extending the longest line so that it separates the butterfly bush from the 'Penelope' roses (B), then planting just the long rectangle. If you want to retain the L-shape and bench in a shorter plan, you can eliminate the southernwood, the 'Frau Dagmar Hartopp' rose (C), and about one-third of the sweet alyssum (F).

Many perennial flowers are very fragrant. Some bearded iris, for example, actually smell like grape soda.

A MEDITERRANEAN GARDEN

Hot, dry summers and infertile, quick-draining soil are characteristic of Mediterranean gardens. These artemisia and jupiter's beard thrive in them.

Blue skies, sunshine, and dry warmth: These are usually the first qualities evoked by the word "Mediterranean." Native plants of the region also contribute to the Mediterranean essence. The foliage often is gray or dull green rather than bright green; many plants have flowers of yellow, blue, or white, mirroring the sunshine, cloudless skies, and bright rocks of the Mediterranean region. And aroma plays a large part: the honeyed scent of broom, the grapelike fragrance of iris, the unique spicy odor of rock rose foliage, and the beloved fragrance that has made lavender famous.

The Mediterranean climate features warm, dry summers and moist, fairly mild winters. In dry-summer regions, this garden will prosper in Zones 8, 9, and 10. In regions where summer combines high temperatures and humidity, the planting will succeed in Zone 8 and the cooler parts of Zone 9. By choosing plants from the alternative selections, gardeners in Zone 7 also can enjoy a fragment of Mediterranean landscape. In all regions, establish the planting in full sun.

Except for the chaste tree and smoke tree, all the plants retain their foliage throughout the year. And with the mixture of gray and differing green leaves, the garden planting will be attractive at all times. Floral interest begins in late winter or early spring with the chartreuse-flowered spurge, then picks up tempo for a peak display in mid- to late spring. In summer, the chaste tree, with cool blue flowers, and smoke tree, with bronzy purple foliage, set the tone, while the anthemis spreads carpets of yellow-centered white daisies, that contrast with the blue of the ground morning glory.

This Mediterranean garden takes little maintenance and uses little water. In fact, in rainy regions it's important to establish

MEDITERRANEAN GARDEN PLANTING PLAN

Scale: 1 square equals 1'

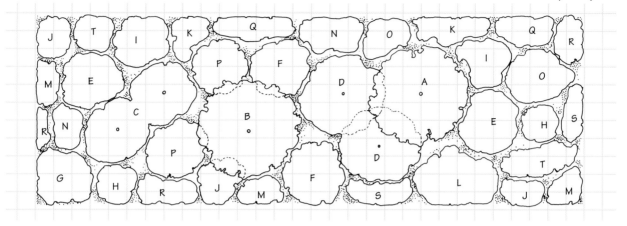

the planting in very well-drained soil. Remove the spent flowering stems of the perennials—iris, spurge, bear's breeches, rose campion, yarrow, and lamb's-ears—as the flowers fade.

The spurge, rose campion, and lamb's-ears reseed throughout the garden. The bulk of the annual maintenance comes in late winter or early spring. Clean out any conspicuous dead leaves and last year's flowering stems, if you haven't already done so. Before the flush of new growth, head back the shrubs and spreading perennials as needed to prevent them from becoming rangy. The rose campion may need replacing every two years; divide and replant the iris and lamb's-ears about every three or four years.

VARIATIONS

The floral color scheme mixes white, yellow tones, and shades of blue, including lavender and violet. To inject a dash of pink, you could replace the white rock rose (E) with one that's clear pink ('Silver Pink'), lilac pink (*Cistus incanus*), or a dark purplish pink ('Brilliancy').

For a shorter rectangular bed, divide the planting down the middle and take either the left or right half, leaving either the side with the smoke tree (A) or the chaste tree (B). Then add 2 feet to the length, planting the edge with your choice of low plants: lamb's-ears, sun rose, yarrow, ground morning glory, marguerite, or wall germander.

MEDITERRANEAN GARDEN PLANTS

A–1–Purple smoke tree (*Cotinus coggygria* 'Purpureus')
B–1–Chaste tree (*Vitex agnus-castus*)
C–2–Jerusalem sage (*Phlomis fruticosa*)
D–2–Bush germander (*Teucrium fruticans*)
E–2–White rock rose (*Cistus* × *corbariensis*)
F–2–Provence broom (*Cytisus purgans*)
G–1–Sageleaf rock rose (*Cistus salviifolius*)
H–2–Spurge (*Euphorbia characias wulfenii*)
I–2–Bear's breeches (*Acanthus mollis*)
J–7–Sweet iris (*Iris pallida* 'Variegata')
K–3–Wall germander (*Teucrium chamaedrys*)
L–2–Green lavender cotton (*Santolina virens*)
M–3–Sun rose, any color (*Helianthemum nummularium*)
N–3–English lavender (*Lavandula angustifolia* 'Hidcote')
O–3–Anthemis (*Anthemis cupaniana*)
P–2–'Powis Castle' artemisia
Q–4–Ground morning glory (*Convolvulus sabatius*)
R–7–Lamb's-ears (*Stachys byzantina*)
S–12–Rose campion (*Lychnis coronaria*)
T–5–Yarrow (*Achillea* 'Taygetea')

ALTERNATIVE SELECTIONS
E–2–Rue (*Ruta graveolens*)
G–3–Evergreen candytuft (*Iberis sempervirens*)
O–2–Lavender cotton (*Santolina chamaecyparissus*)

Lamb's-ears is a natural for Mediterranean gardens. These robust perennials actually remain healthier in a dry climate than they do in a wet one. Their fuzzy silver leaves are attractive at all times. Stalks of tiny purple flowers appear in midsummer.

A BIRD GARDEN

Birds are drawn to gardens that offer food, drink, and places to spend the night. Berries, seeds, and insects constitute food; water is the drink. Shelter can be a variety of plants allowed to grow together in an unmanicured fashion that mimics the natural landscape. Important to the design of a bird planting is the edging effect that you see in a forest clearing, where shrubs of various heights bridge the transition from tree to grassland.

This plan for a bird corner includes a little of everything that a wide variety of birds find appealing. Berry-eating birds will gravitate to the serviceberry, Washington hawthorn, rose, burning bush, dogwood, honeysuckle, and—late in the season—the cotoneaster, barberry, and bearberry. Seedeaters will flock to the sunflowers, goldenrod, and fountain grass. Birds that favor insects will seek out the fare on Washington hawthorn, rose, and pyracantha. Even hummingbirds will be tempted into the garden, drawn by the blossoms of the honeysuckle and coral bells.

Birdbaths are a universal lure for bathing

Birds will flock to your garden if you plant flowers, shrubs, and herbs they find attractive. Look for plants that produce nectar, seeds, berries, or safe shelter.

and drinking; a pathway of gravel or plain earth encourages dust baths. And the intertwining shrub growth, some of it thorny, provides safe bird nesting sites.

Although this planting is aimed at satisfying the specific needs of birds, you'll find it is visually attractive as well, with colorful flowers or fruit appearing in all seasons. Several of the shrubs also display impressive fall color before shedding their leaves for the year.

The main planting list is suitable in Zones 5, 6, and 7, where winter cold rules out many broad-leaved evergreen trees and shrubs. In Zone 8, use the main list or any of the plants given in the alternative selections list. In Zone 9 and dry-summer Zone 10, where winter temperatures are mild, be sure to use the alternative selections.

Because birds are attracted to naturalistic plantings, yearly maintenance is minimal. Let leaf litter accumulate as much as your sense of neatness will allow: Birds will forage in it for insects and seeds. In late winter or early spring, cut last year's spent black-eyed Susan stems and those of goldenrod and the fountain grass. If the seeds haven't already been dispersed or eaten by the birds, shake them out on the ground. When the soil warms, set out new sunflower plants. Prune shrubs only as needed to correct wayward or unbalanced growth.

VARIATIONS

The larger the planting, the more inviting it is to birds. However, you can reduce the size of the garden and still present an alluring assortment of plants. Draw a line between the redtwig dogwood (F) and sunflower (M), and plant only the part that contains the redtwig dogwood. For a less abrupt edge, add 3 feet to the "cut edge" of the planting and wrap the goldenrod (L) (adding five more plants) around the end of the dogwood.

BIRD GARDEN PLANTING PLAN

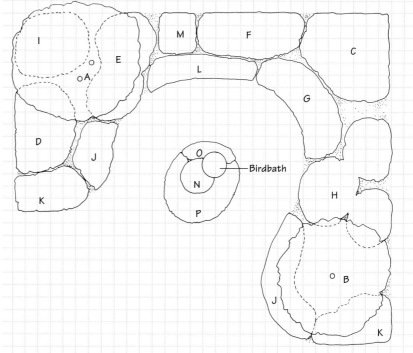

Scale: 1 square equals 1'

BIRD GARDEN PLANTS

A–2–Washington hawthorn (*Crataegus phaenopyrum*)
B–1–Apple serviceberry (*Amelanchier × grandiflora*)
C–1–Colorado spruce (*Picea pungens* 'Fat Albert')
D–2–'Ballerina' rose
E–2–Dwarf burning bush (*Euonymus alatus* 'Compactus')
F–2–Redtwig dogwood (*Cornus alba* 'Sibirica')
G–2–Rockspray cotoneaster (*Cotoneaster horizontalis*)
H–3–Japanese barberry (*Berberis thunbergii*)
I–1–Tatarian honeysuckle (*Lonicera tatarica*)
J–26–Black-eyed Susan (*Rudbeckia fulgida* 'Goldsturm')
K–8–Red-osier dogwood (*Cornus sericea* 'Kelseyi')
L–10–Goldenrod (*Solidago × *'Cloth of Gold')
M–9–Common sunflower (*Helianthus annuus*)
N–5–Fountain grass (*Pennisetum alopecuroides*)
O–8–Coral bells (*Heuchera sanguinea*)
P–6–Bearberry (*Arctostaphylos uva-ursi*)

ALTERNATIVE SELECTIONS
B–1–Purple-leaf sand cherry (*Prunus × cistena*)
C–1–Firethorn (*Pyracantha coccinea*)
E–2–European cranberrybush (*Viburnum opulus* 'Compactum')
F–2–Japanese privet (*Ligustrum japonicum* 'Texanum')
H–3–Chinese holly (*Ilex cornuta* 'Berries Jubilee')
K–8–Oregon grapeholly (*Mahonia aquifolium* 'Compacta')
N–5–Purple fountain grass (*Pennisetum setaceum*)

Winter is a hard time for songbirds such as cardinals. Keep them happy by leaving seed-laden flower stalks in place during the winter.

A HUMMINGBIRD GARDEN

Hummingbirds possess a universal charm. Their iridescent plumage immediately attracts attention, and their unique method of flight and overall panache inspire wonder and admiration. A staple of the hummingbird's diet is flower nectar—nature's sugar solution—which supplies energy for the birds' incessant motion. A sure way to attract hummingbirds, then, is to offer an abundance of their favorite nectar-bearing flowers, ideally in a part of your garden sheltered from the wind.

Brightly colored flowers are a powerful hummingbird attractant. Red and orange shades are the birds' favorite colors, though they give blue and pink a share of attention. Funnel-shaped and tubular blossoms also pique the birds' curiosity, offering the hope of nectar at the base of the flowers.

The plants in this hummingbird garden, therefore, focus on the red sector of the spectrum, from the orange butterfly weed to the red-purple butterfly bush, and including the warm pink shades of summer phlox, coral bells, and foxglove. Flowering starts in spring with coral bells, scarlet trumpet or goldflame honeysuckle, and foxglove; reaches a peak in summer; then fades in fall with the last blooms of scarlet sage, petunia, flowering tobacco, and beard-tongue.

Several varieties of hummingbirds frequent gardens in the West and Southwest; east of the plains, only one, the ruby-throated hummingbird, visits during the year's warmer months. The main plant list covers eastern and western gardens in Zones 5 through 9; plants in the alternative list can be used in western Zone 9 and should be used in dry-summer Zone 10.

As soon as the weather permits gardening in late winter or early spring, clean up the planting, removing dead leaves and the spent plants of last year's annuals: flowering tobacco, petunias, and scarlet sage. Cut back the old flowering stems of the perennials: beard-tongue, foxglove, summer phlox, and bee balm. Prune the butterfly bush to 6 to 12 inches from the ground. Thin and train the scarlet trumpet or goldflame honeysuckle as needed. Head back any wayward growth on the weigela, but wait until after it has flowered to prune it for size. When the soil

HUMMINGBIRD GARDEN PLANTS

A–1–Scarlet trumpet honeysuckle (Lonicera × brownii 'Dropmore Scarlet')

B–1–Weigela (Weigela florida 'Bristol Ruby')

C–1–Common butterfly bush (Buddleia davidii 'Nanho Purple')

D–1–Butterfly weed (Asclepias tuberosa)

E–13–Common beard-tongue (Penstemon barbatus 'Prairie Fire')

F–17–Coral bells (Heuchera sanguinea)

G–3–Torch lily (Kniphofia uvaria)

H–7–Strawberry foxglove (Digitalis × mertonensis)

I–3–Bee balm (Monarda didyma 'Cambridge Scarlet')

J–14–Flowering tobacco (Nicotiana alata, red or pink)

K–16–Petunia (Petunia × hybrida red selection)

L–4–Summer phlox (Phlox paniculata, orange or red cultivar, such as 'Orange Perfection')

M–10–Scarlet sage (Salvia splendens)

ALTERNATIVE SELECTIONS

A–1–Goldflame honeysuckle (Lonicera × heckrottii)

B–1–Common butterfly bush (Buddleia davidii)

C–1–Autumn sage (Salvia greggii)

E–13–Columbine (Aquilegia, long-spurred hybrid)

I–1–Scarlet monkeyflower (Mimulus cardinalis)

L–5–California fuschia (Zauschneria California)

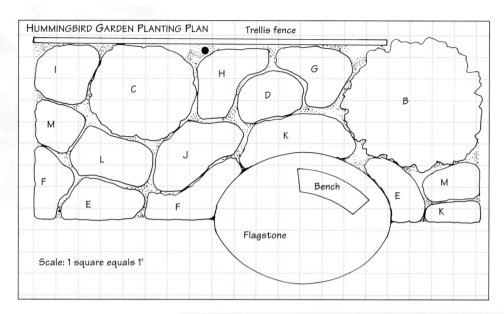

HUMMINGBIRD GARDEN PLANTING PLAN — Trellis fence

I, C, M, H, G, D, B, K, L, J, F, E, F, Bench, E, M, K, Flagstone

Scale: 1 square equals 1'

warms and frost danger has passed, set out new plants of the annuals.

VARIATIONS

The recommended plants play to the hummingbird's favorite color: red. If this scheme is too vibrant for your taste, you can alter it by choosing alternative colors. Use a pink-flowered beard-tongue, such as 'Prairie Splendor'; a pink-flowered bee balm, such as 'Croftway Pink'; a white-flowering tobacco; pink, blue, or purple selections of petunia; pink or lavender cultivars of summer phlox; or violet-flowered scarlet sage.

The crimson flowers of scarlet trumpet vine are a favorite of hummingbirds. Train this vigorous vine over a sturdy trellis or arbor.

Hummingbirds prefer tubular-shaped red blooms. One of the best is 'Lady in Red' Texas sage. It grows 2 feet tall and blooms all summer long.

A BUTTERFLY GARDEN

Who can be unmoved by butterflies? Like fragile works of art, they lazily float in and out of gardens on warm, sunny days, searching for food in nectar-laden blossoms. Species of butterflies vary from one part of the country to another. A sure way to lure them to your own garden, no matter where you live, is to plant their favorite flowers.

This butterfly garden brings together 13 plants known for their appeal to butterflies. The flowering starts in mid- to late spring with the catmint. In mid- to late summer, it peaks with the tall Joe-Pye weed, common butterfly bush, and butterfly weed dominating the show. It then continues into fall, until cool weather calls a halt.

Establish this bed in full sun, perhaps in a lawn, and give plants routine watering. Gardeners in Zones 5 through 9 can use plants in the main list; dry-summer Zone 10 gardeners should choose the alternative selections, replacing the Joe-Pye weed with lantana and the spirea with white Jupiter's beard.

A standard cleanup, in late winter or early spring, is the major maintenance for the year. Clear out dead leaves, dead plants of last year's flowering tobacco, and spent flowering stems on the perennials. Cut back the butterfly bush to 6 to 12 inches from the ground, and cut back the English lavender, spirea, and catmint by about half. Eventually, you will need to dig up most of the perennials in early spring and divide them to rejuvenate the plantings. First among these, after several years, will be the black-eyed Susan, both forms of coreopsis, and the common yarrow.

VARIATIONS

If you want a smaller, shallower bed, you can cut the planting in half. Divide the plan by drawing a line between the dots, and plant whichever half appeals more to you. To attract a variety of butterflies it's also important to include food plants for their larvae. Dill, fennel, carrot, and parsley are all popular food plants for butterfly species. Wild plants such as nettle, milkweed, clover, and violet are also attractive to butterfly larvae.

BUTTERFLY GARDEN PLANTS

A–1–Common butterfly bush (Buddleia davidii)

B–2–Joe-Pye weed (Eupatorium maculatum)

C–3–Butterfly weed (Asclepias tuberosa)

D–4–English lavender (Lavandula angustifolia)

E–5–'Autumn Joy' Sedum

F–9–Common yarrow (Achillea millefolium)

G–6–Catmint (Nepeta × faassenii)

H–3–Spirea (Spiraea japonica 'Anthony Waterer')

I–3–Lanceleaf coreopsis (Coreopsis lanceolata)

J–5–Threadleaf coreopsis (Coreopsis verticillata 'Moonbeam')

K–6–Daylily (Hemerocallis, yellow-flowered cultivar)

L–15–Flowering tobacco (Nicotiana alata)

M–6–Black-eyed Susan (Rudbeckia fulgida 'Goldsturm')

ALTERNATIVE SELECTIONS

B–2–Lantana (Lantana camara)

H–7–White Jupiter's beard (Centranthus ruber 'Albus')

BUTTERFLY GARDEN PLANTING PLAN

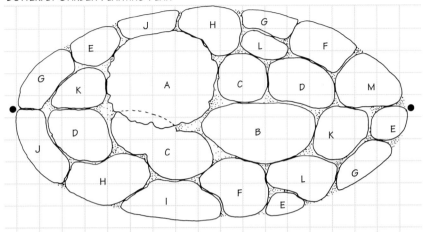

Scale: 1 square equals 1'

Variety is the secret to butterflies. The more flowers you grow, the more butterflies you will see. Be sure to include plants for the larvae too.

Butterfly bush will attract a wide variety of butterflies to your garden. This tender perennial shrub grows quickly and is highly fragrant.

A MINIATURE GARDEN

One of the greatest reasons for "gardening small" has always been limited space. Now, with the hastening pace of life and multiple demands on time, an increasingly important reason is the lack of time to devote to gardening. Small-garden planning, however, raises an immediate choice: Should you quickly fill the space with a few normal-sized plants, or spend time tracking down naturally small plants that you can combine to create a varied, scaled-down landscape?

For the real gardening enthusiast, there's really no choice. This planting scheme presents an assortment of attractive, easy-to-grow plants in a miniature landscape that will provide interest throughout the growing season in a space only 12 feet long by 5 feet wide. Children interested in starting a garden may find this a rewarding project.

This garden was designed for full sun in Zones 5 through 9 and dry-summer Zone 10. Four of the five alternative selections are optional choices for gardeners in Zones 9 and 10; the jade plant choice is for Zone 10 only.

Because the plants themselves are small and feature small flowers and fine-textured foliage, this planting looks better in a raised bed. Use railroad ties, construction timbers, or two or more courses of brick to make a slightly raised planting, which will show off the garden. Plants should have well-drained, reasonably good garden soil and routine garden watering.

Just in advance of the growing season, in late winter or early spring, tidy up the planting. Remove the dead leaves and any spent stems of last year's flowers. Cut back the roses and evergreen candytuft by about half, and trim any plants that are encroaching on their neighbors. Head back any rangy stems on the mugo pine to maintain compactness, cutting them back to branching stems or to the base of a year's growth. During the growing season, groom the planting to keep it neat. In Zones 5, 6, and 7, apply a winter protection of evergreen boughs or salt hay in late fall or as soon as the ground freezes; this will offset the freeze-thaw cycles that can damage raised-bed plantings in cold regions.

MINIATURE GARDEN PLANTS

A–1–Mugo pine (Pinus mugo var. mugo)
B–5–Miniature hybrid rose, such as 'Popcorn' or 'Rosemarin'
C–10–Evergreen candytuft (Iberis sempervirens 'Autumn Beauty')
D–3–Dalmatian bellflower (Campanula portenschlagiana)
E–3–Wall rockcress (Arabis caucasica)
F–7–Dianthus 'Tiny Rubies'
G–4–Woolly thyme (Thymus pseudolanuginosus)
H–5–Blue fescue (Festuca glauca)
I–2–Stonecrop (Sedum spathulifolium)
J–2–Mt. Atlas Daisy (Anacyclus depressus)
K–Irish moss (Sagina subulata)—1 or 2 flats: 2-inch squares cut and planted 6 inches apart

ALTERNATIVE SELECTIONS

A–1–Variegated jade plant (Crassula Ovata 'Compacta Variegata')
D–2–Serbian bellflower (Campanula poscharskyana)
E–3–Alpine geranium (Erodium reichardii)
H–10–Rhodohypoxis (Rhodohypoxis baurii)
J–2–New Zealand brass buttons (Leptinella squalida)

MINIATURE GARDEN PLANTING PLAN

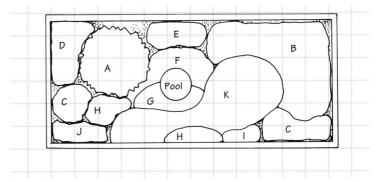

Scale: 1 square equals 1'

VARIATIONS

This planting was designed to be the specified size, but you can vary the color scheme by selecting different cultivars. Instead of the suggested white or pink roses and 'Tiny Rubies' dianthus, you could select a crimson dianthus such as 'Zing Rose' and a red miniature rose, or choose a scarlet selection of hardy carnation (Dianthus caryophyllus), which would contrast brightly with an orange or yellow rose. Reliable carnation varieties include 'Snowfire', 'Cheyenne', 'King of Blacks', and 'Arctic Fire'.

Small-scale perennials such as dianthus are ideal for miniature gardens.

Other good choices for small gardens are dwarf conifers, grasses, mosses, heaths, heathers, and ground covers.

A KITCHEN GARDEN

Herbs,
vegetables,
roses, and
annuals mingle
in this inviting
kitchen garden.
The garden
includes a
range of plants
for cutting and
eating.

Like the apothecary garden (see pages 52 and 53), the kitchen garden traces its roots to medieval times and beyond, when communities had to be self-sufficient. Apothecary plants were used to treat bodily ailments; kitchen plants provided edibles of all sorts to nurture the body. Nowadays, the most common planting of edibles is the vegetable garden. This kitchen garden scheme returns to the older concept. It includes not only vegetables but also culinary herbs and fruit crops, as well as meets the contemporary desire for fresh flowers in the home by including an assortment of productive annuals and a perennial for cutting.

The plants in the larger bed are those that would be used frequently but in small quantities: culinary herbs; tomatoes and green onions for salads and garnishes; strawberries and apples or pears for special desserts; and productive annuals for colorful bouquets. The smaller bed features additional flowers for cutting, though some of this space can be

KITCHEN GARDEN PLANTS

A–1–Apple (Malus pumila) or pear (Pyrus communis), espaliered tree on dwarfing rootstock
B–5–Strawberry (Fragaria × ananassa)
C–1–Garden sage (Salvia officinalis)
D–6–Chives (Allium schoenoprasum)
E–1–Common thyme (Thymus vulgaris) or Silver thyme (Thymus vulgaris 'Argenteus') or Lemon thyme (Thymus × citriodorus)
F–2–Oregano (Origanum vulgare)
G–12–Parsley (Petroselinum crispum)
H–4–Sweet basil (Ocimum basilicum)
I–18–Green onion
J–2–Tomato
K–6–African marigold (Tagetes erecta) or Snapdragon (Antirrhinum majus) or Zinnia (Zinnia elegans)
L–36–French marigold (Tagetes patula)
M–6–Shasta daisy (Leucanthemum × superbum)
N–6–Pot marigold (Calendula officinalis, orange selection)
O–6–Pot marigold (Calendula officinalis, yellow selection)

ALTERNATIVE SELECTIONS
N–1–Zucchini
O–1–Crookneck squash

KITCHEN GARDEN PLANTING PLAN

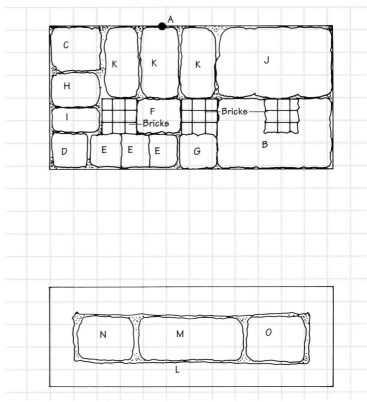

Scale: 1 square equals 1'

converted to vegetables, using the alternative selections. Good, well-drained soil, routine garden watering, and full sun during the growing season will give you a flourishing kitchen garden in Zones 5 through 9 and dry-summer Zone 10. Choose the fruit tree, strawberry, and tomato cultivars that are best suited to your particular climate.

Maintenance is concentrated in late winter and early spring: a little pruning and trimming plus replacement of annual plants and any herbs that may have perished over the winter. Prune the espaliered fruit tree as needed to maintain its form. Cut back by up to half the garden sage, oregano, and thymes. When the soil is workable, set out green onion starts, parsley seedlings, and pot marigolds; set out the tomatoes, sweet basil, African and French marigolds, zinnia, and snapdragon when the soil has warmed.

In the larger bed, switch the tomatoes and annual flowers each year to avoid exposing the tomatoes to soil-borne diseases. During the growing season, watch the espaliered fruit tree's growth: Train new growth to follow the espalier pattern and cut out wayward stems.

VARIATIONS

If the double-bed plan doesn't suit your space or needs, plant only the larger rectangle with its assortment of edibles and flowers. If you want the two beds but prefer more vegetables, consider the small-bed options in the alternative selections list, substituting zucchini and crookneck squash for the orange and yellow pot marigolds.

A versatile flower for kitchen gardens is nasturtiums. Their flowers and leaves have a peppery flavor that adds color and zip to salads.

A CUTTING GARDEN

F ew things in everyday life are as uplifting as a bouquet of fresh flowers. What, then, could be more satisfying than picking them from your own garden? Although you can cut virtually any flower for arrangements, not all have a long vase life. The annuals and perennials in this planting scheme are both attractive and fairly long-lasting as cut flowers. The bells of Ireland, sea lavender, fern-leaf yarrow, baby's breath, and strawflower can be harvested and dried for later use as components of everlasting floral arrangements as well.

A cutting garden can provide fresh, colorful flowers all season long. This one includes spider flower, melampodium, blue salvia, and marigold.

In spring, the garden will offer pot marigolds, snapdragons, and Shasta daisies, but the flowering peak occurs in midsummer, when virtually the entire cutting garden bed will be bursting with bright color. Flowering continues into fall until the first frost with purple coneflower and false sunflower. The alternative selections are options for varying the color of the garden. With one exception, the plants in both lists will grow in Zones 4 through 9 and dry-summer Zone 10.

The exception is the carnation, which you may need to treat as an annual in Zones 4, 5, and 6, because it probably won't survive the winters in those zones. Be sure to place this cutting garden in full sun and give it "vegetable garden care"—good soil and a regular water supply during the growing season.

This garden's yearly maintenance starts in late winter or early spring, when you need to clear the garden of last year's spent annual plants and the old flowering stems and dead leaves of the perennials. Where the annuals had been, dig the soil, adding a little fertilizer and new organic amendments. Then, when the frost danger has passed, set out new annuals. Among the perennials, the baby's breath can remain in place permanently. But about every three years in early spring, you will need to dig and divide the coneflowers, fern-leaf

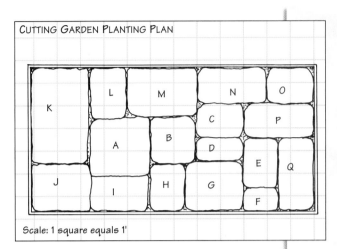

CUTTING GARDEN PLANTING PLAN

Scale: 1 square equals 1'

CUTTING GARDEN PLANTS

A–1–Baby's breath (Gypsophila paniculata 'Bristol Fairy')
B–4–Purple coneflower (Echinacea purpurea)
C–4–Fern-leaf yarrow (Achillea filipendulina 'Coronation Gold')
D–2–False sunflower (Heliopsis helianthoides scabra)
E–4–Shasta daisy (Leucanthemum × superbum)
F–2–Carnation (Dianthus caryophyllus)
G–6–Flowering tobacco (Nicotiana alata)
H–6–Snapdragon (Antirrhinum majus)
I–6–Sea lavender (Limonium latifolium)
J–6–Scarlet sage (Salvia splendens 'Flare')
K–8–Triploid marigold (Tagetes, triploid hybrid)
L–4–Bells of Ireland (Moluccella laevis)
M–6–Zinnia (Zinnia elegans)
N–6–Pot marigold (Calendula officinalis)
O–6–French marigold (Tagetes patula)
P–6–Cockscomb (Celosia argentea cristata 'Plumosa')
Q–8–Scarlet sage (Salvia splendens 'Sizzler Hybrids')

ALTERNATIVE SELECTIONS
B–4–Black-eyed Susan (Rudbeckia 'Goldsturm')
D–2–Yellow cosmos (Cosmos sulphureus, 'Klondike' strain)
J–4–Yellow cosmos (Cosmos sulphureus, 'Dwarf Klondike' strain)
L–6–Strawflower (Helichrysum bracteatum)
N–6–Blanket flower (Gaillardia pulchella)

yarrow, and false sunflower. The Shasta daisy may need dividing every other year. Even in the zones where the carnation will live from year to year, periodically you'll need to start new plants from cuttings when the old plants become woody and less productive.

During the flowering season, routinely remove spent flowers left on the plants after cuttings for bouquets have been taken; this prevents the plants from setting seed, which causes a decline in bloom production.

VARIATIONS

Because a cutting garden is essentially a flower factory, these rectangular plant units are perfect for easy care and cutting, yet they avoid the row-crop look of a vegetable garden. This setup also makes it easy to alter the garden's size by eliminating certain blocks of plants. You could, for example, gain a shorter bed by leaving out the marigolds and scarlet sage (K and J). Or, to create a nearly square bed, you might want to eliminate the blocks of Shasta daisy, carnation, scarlet sage, cockscomb, French marigold, and one-third of the pot marigold (E, F, Q, P, O, and N). Many other alterations can be made by slightly changing the number of plants in a block.

Gladiolus would also be a good alternate selection. Treated properly, their tall, spectacular flower spikes will last for two weeks in a bouquet. Color choice is almost limitless.

GARDENS FOR SPECIAL SITUATIONS

The toughest landscape problems can be solved when you have a good garden plan to work with. Slopes, deep shade, dry, exposed locations, and wet spots can become garden assets when you plant trees, shrubs, and flowers that are capable of handling these conditions.

The secret to success is to work in tandem with nature instead of against it. For example, if you dream of having a perfect lawn but your backyard is heavily shaded, don't try to grow turfgrasses. Instead, opt for shade-loving perennials and ground covers.

In this chapter you'll find innovative planting solutions for a wide range of backyard challenges.

Even the most uninviting garden corner can be revived with careful planning. This shady garden was bare before it was rejuvenated with shade-loving plants.

A SHADE GARDEN

Gardeners often regard a shaded yard as a limitation, knowing that it is a poor location for such favorites as roses, irises, peonies, and a host of seasonal annuals. But all it takes is a changed view to welcome this shade garden of azaleas, hostas, and astilbes.

Shade comes in various forms. Light shade is the brightest; it comes through lattice or an open-canopied tree. At the other extreme is the dense shade found under a heavy foliage canopy. The amount of shade also varies from partial (morning sun, afternoon shade) to day-long. Even day-long shade ranges in degree from the fairly light form cast by shadows of tall trees or buildings to the gloom in a narrow passage between buildings. The beds in this garden are shaded by the canopies of the dogwoods (or evergreen pears) included in the planting scheme. In an already shady spot, you can omit the trees without affecting the design. The main plant list will serve Zones 5 through 9, though gardeners in Zones 7 and 8 can choose from the broad range of azaleas available in their local nurseries. The alternative selections should be used in Zone 10 and may be considered for Zone 9 gardens. The alternative azaleas, in particular, are more suitable for Zone 9 gardens than the azaleas on the main list. In all areas, see that the planting receives routine garden watering.

Varied foliage and flower colors make this planting attractive from early spring until frost spells an end to the growing year. Lenten roses and violets usher in the flowering season, followed by azaleas, brunnera, bleeding heart, bloodroot, and foxglove. In late spring and summer, Serbian bellflower, astilbe, and summersweet provide a burst of color; hostas bloom too, although most are not especially showy. Overhead, the kousa dogwoods spread clouds of color. The season finishes in fall with the Japanese anemone and the colorful foliage of the azalea and dogwood.

The time for maintenance is late winter or early spring, before the year's growth begins in earnest. Clean out the dead leaves and trim the spent flowering stems of last year's perennials. Prune the summersweet if it is growing out of bounds or, if you are using the alternative list, cut back the hydrangea by at least half. Wait until just after flowering to shape the azaleas. If the Serbian bellflower, Japanese anemone, or brunnera are spreading too far, dig out the excess plants.

Electrify shady spots in your landscape with perennial flowers that thrive in low light. Hosta and astilbe are two dependable shade lovers.

SHADE GARDEN PLANTS

A–2–Kousa dogwood (Cornus kousa)
B–2–Pink-shell azalea (Rhododendron vaseyi)
C–4–Royal azalea (Rhododendron schlippenbachii)
D–3–Azalea (Rhododendron 'Northern Lights')
E–1–Summersweet (Clethra alnifolia)
F–4–Ostrich fern (Matteuccia struthiopteris)
G–7–Lenten rose (Helleborus orientalis)
H–3–Siebold hosta (Hosta sieboldiana)
I–10–Strawberry foxglove (Digitalis × mertonensis)
J–10–Wavy hosta (Hosta 'Mediovariegata')
K–2–Astilbe (Astilbe 'Red Sentinel')
L–7–Brunnera (Brunnera macrophylla)
M–6–Old-fashioned bleeding heart (Dicentra spectabilis)
N–1–'Piedmont Gold' Hosta
O–7–Spotted dead nettle (Lamium maculatum
　'White Nancy')
P–4–Sweet violet (Viola odorata)
Q–2–Bigleaf ligularia (Ligularia dentata 'Desdemona')
R–8–Serbian bellflower (Campanula poscharskyana)
S–2–Bloodroot (Sanguinaria canadensis)
T–4–Japanese anemone (Anemone japonica)

ALTERNATIVE SELECTIONS
A–2–Evergreen pear (Pyrus kawakamii)
B–2–Azalea (Rhododendron 'Nova Zembla')
C–4–Azalea (Rhododendron 'Chionoipes')
D–3–Azalea (Rhododendron 'Sherwood Orchid')
E–1–Bigleaf hydrangea (Hydrangea macrophylla 'Tricolor')
F–5–Southern sword fern (Nephrolepis cordifolia)
H–3–Kaffir lily (Clivia miniata)
J–12–Variegated lilyturf (Liriope muscari 'Variegata')
K–3–Japanese anemone (Anemone japonica)
M–10–Columbine (Aquilegia 'McKenna Hybrids')
N–3–Common calla lily (Zantedeschia aethiopica 'Minor')
Q–2–Ligularia (Ligularia tussilaginea 'Aureo-maculata')
S–5–Polyanthus primrose (Primula × polyantha)

VARIATIONS

This shaded garden is planned as a woodland walk, perhaps along a mossy stone path or under a canopy of tall deciduous trees. However, if your space is limited, either the large or small portion of the planting can stand by itself.

Old-fashioned bleeding heart pops up in early spring and makes a lovely companion for large-leaved hostas and late tulips. In midsummer this reliable perennial goes dormant until the following spring.

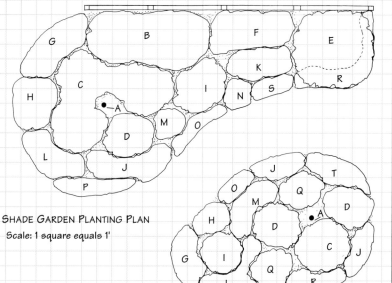

SHADE GARDEN PLANTING PLAN
Scale: 1 square equals 1'

A WATER-THRIFTY GARDEN

Some perennials are naturally able to survive drought and heat. These daylilies, Russian sage, black-eyed Susan, Joe-Pye weed, and ornamental grasses are among them.

Many favorite garden plants need a regular supply of water to look their best. If rainfall during the growing season doesn't provide enough, the gardener must water them regularly. Watering poses a problem if you can't always be there when needed with the hose or if you're trying to conserve water. The solution is to find attractive plants that flourish on limited water.

This planting scheme features an assortment of water-thrifty plants that thrive in Zones 5 through 9; gardeners in dry-summer Zone 10 should use the alternative selections, and gardeners in dry-summer Zone 9 may choose from either list. Most of the color comes from the flowers, but three plants—Japanese barberry, lamb's-ears, and fountain grass—offer colored foliage rather than showy blossoms. In the main planting, flowers are concentrated in summer and early fall. A garden containing the alternative selections will have a slightly longer flowering period. It will start in spring with the rock rose, bush morning glory, and Mexican daisy and continue well into fall with the Mexican bush sage.

In all areas, establish the bed in well-drained soil where plants will receive full sun. Although these plants can take some dryness between waterings, just how much water they'll need depends on your climate: temperature, rainfall, wind, and cloud cover. You can be sure, however, that they'll be standing tall when roses, snapdragons, and lawn start to droop.

A basic spring cleaning (in late winter or early spring) gets the garden set for the year. Clear out the dead leaves, and cut down the spent flower stems on the perennials. Cut back the catmint and English lavender by about half, and cut back the Russian sage to about 6 inches. Lightly prune the Japanese barberry as needed to keep it from encroaching on neighboring plants.

VARIATIONS

If space is limited, you can cut the planting in half. Draw a line from the back of the bed to the front between the fern-leaf yarrow (C) and the Japanese barberry (A); plant the half that contains the fern-leaf yarrow, reducing the numbers of cupid's-dart (H) (or the alternative vervain) to three and the lamb's-ears (L) also to three.

WATER-THRIFTY GARDEN PLANTS

A–1–Japanese barberry (*Berberis thunbergii*)
B–2–Russian sage (*Perovskia atriplicifolia*)
C–6–Fern-leaf yarrow (*Achillea filipendulina* 'Coronation Gold')
D–3–Fountain grass (*Pennisetum alopecuroides*)
E–6–Purple coneflower (*Echinacea purpurea* 'Magnus')
F–6–Black-eyed Susan (*Rudbeckia fulgida* 'Goldsturm')
G–3–Butterfly weed (*Asclepias tuberosa*)
H–5–Cupid's dart (*Catananche caerulea*)
I–2–Cushion spurge (*Euphorbia polychroma*)
J–3–Blazing star (*Liatris spicata* 'Kobold')
K–4–Yarrow (*Achillea* 'Moonshine')
L–6–Lamb's-ears (*Stachys byzantina* 'Silver Carpet')
M–2–Cinquefoil (*Potentilla* 'Abbotswood')
N–3–Lanceleaf coreopsis (*Coreopsis lanceolata* 'Goldfink')
O–4–Catmint (*Nepeta* × *faassenii*)

ALTERNATIVE SELECTIONS
A–1–Crimson-spot rock rose (*Cistus ladanifer*)
B–2–Mexican bush sage (*Salvia leucantha*)
D–3–Purple fountain grass (*Pennisetum setaceum* 'Atrosanguineum')
G–3–Gaura (*Gaura lindheimeri*)
H–2–Vervain (*Verbena rigida*)
I–2–Sea lavender (*Limonium latifolium*)
J–1–Bush morning glory (*Convolvulus cneorum*)
M–4–English lavender (*Lavandula angustifolia* 'Hidcote')
O–2–Mexican daisy (*Erigeron karvinskianus*)

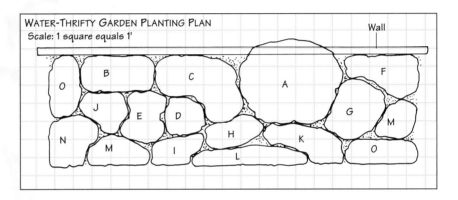

WATER-THRIFTY GARDEN PLANTING PLAN
Scale: 1 square equals 1'
Wall

Other good alternate plants include yarrow and perennial blue salvia. They are a dynamic duo that can take the heat and keep right on blooming. After the flower show fades, prune both plants back and enjoy a second wave of bloom later in the season.

A DAMP-SOIL GARDEN

Hosta, foxglove, and lady's mantle are three perennials that will thrive in wet, poorly drained soil.

Most familiar garden plants thrive in well-drained soil; during active growth their roots need abundant air. Poorly drained soil contains little air in its pores so few plants grow in it. However, a few perennials have adapted to stream- and pond-side growing conditions. They are a good choice for low wet spots in a garden.

This planting includes some of the most attractive moisture-loving plants. Although some grow well in drier situations, most do best with constantly moist soil.

Flowering begins in early to mid-spring with the sky-blue blooms of forget-me-not and lasts into fall with the red and blue cardinal flowers (or the alternative New England aster). Never an eye-jolting blast of mass color, this bed is nonetheless always interesting; its varied foliage textures and colors are punctuated by flowers in yellow, red, pink, purple, and blue. The alternative selections give you the chance to vary the planting palette.

In cool-summer regions, place the bed in full sun; but in warmer areas, locate the garden where it will receive light shade during the hottest part of the day. Because wet sites are found most often in climates with frequent rainfall during the spring and summer growing seasons, these plants were chosen for moist-summer Zones 5 through 9.

In late winter or early spring, before the perennials break dormancy, go over the bed, removing the dead leaves and spent flowering stems from the previous year. After several years you may need to dig up and divide the bee balm, cardinal flower, and New England aster.

VARIATIONS

This bed was designed to be an irregular island, perhaps surrounded by lawn in the low spot of a garden. However, if you need an irregular bed that will fit against a wall or fence, draw a line between the dots at either end of the plan and plant the larger portion, using just two yellow flag iris.

DAMP-SOIL GARDEN PLANTING PLAN

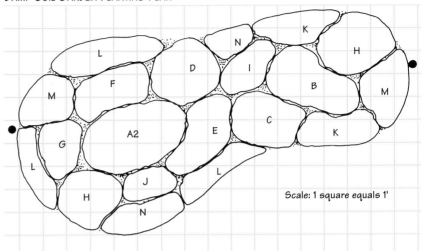

Scale: 1 square equals 1'

DAMP-SOIL GARDEN PLANTS

A–2–Queen-of-the-prairie (*Filipendula rubra* 'Venusta')
B–4–Yellow flag iris (*Iris pseudacorus*)
C–1–Narrow-spiked ligularia (*Ligularia stenocephala* 'The Rocket')
D–1–Ligularia (*Ligularia dentata* 'Desdemona')
E–3–Yellow flag (*Iris psendacorus*)
F–3–Cardinal flower (*Lobelia cardinalis*)
G–2–Columbine meadow rue (*Thalictrum aquilegifolium*)
H–5–Globeflower (*Trollius europaeus* 'Superbus')
I–2–Bee balm (*Monarda didyma* 'Violet Queen')
J–2–Spiderwort (*Tradescantia virginiana*)
K–8–Variegated purple moor grass (*Molinia caerulea* 'Variegata')
L–10–Forget-me-not (*Myosotis scorpioides*)
M–4–Siebold hosta (*Hosta sieboldiana*)
N–3–Lance leave hosta (*Hosta* 'Lancifolia')

ALTERNATIVE SELECTIONS
A–2–Goatsbeard (*Aruncus dioicus*)
C–3–New England aster (*Aster novae-angliae*)
E–2–Purple loosestrife (*Lythrum salicaria* 'Morden's Pink')
E–2–Cardinal flower (*Lobelia gerardii* 'Vedrariensis') for zones 8 and 9
I–2–Bee balm (*Monarda didyma* 'Cambridge Scarlet')

New England aster comes in several colors and blooms in late summer and early fall. It is a native wildflower that can tolerate both dry and wet soil conditions. Monarch butterflies love this late bloomer.

A POND GARDEN

From ancient times, water has been an essential element in pleasure gardens. Now, as then, its effect is more than coolness: Water is able to soothe or pacify, even impart a sense of rejuvenation. And it doesn't take a great body of water to accomplish this. The Persians, Moors, and Japanese all were masters of effect with small pools and channels, often employing the sound of moving or splashing water to enhance the impression of serenity.

This pond garden is deliberately small, a tranquil pool to tuck into a garden corner. The plants complement the restful scene with flowers in delicate hues, and if they are not true pond-edge denizens, they at least look as though they could be.

Plants in the main list are suited to Zones 5 through 9. The alternative selections should be chosen for Zone 10 gardens and can be used as options in Zone 9. Where summers are cool, the planting will thrive in full sun,

but in warm- to hot-summer regions, it should receive light shade, at least during the hottest part of the day. In all areas, see that the plants receive routine watering to supplement rainfall.

When gardening weather returns in late winter or early spring, clean up the dead leaves, and cut back last year's feather reed grass foliage before new growth begins. You can leave most of the plants in place for many years with no attention beyond cleanup and watering. But when the ajuga and spotted dead nettle become patchy, dig, divide, and replant them in early spring.

VARIATIONS

If you have a smaller space and want more of the pool margin exposed, you can eliminate the shorter "arm" by stopping the planting where the ligularia (D) meets the yellow flag iris (C).

POND GARDEN PLANTS

A–4–Feather reed grass (Calamagrostis
  acutiflora 'Stricta')
B–5–Heart-leaf bergenia (Bergenia cordifolia)
C–6–Yellow flag iris (Iris pseudacorus)
D–2–Ligularia (Ligularia dentata 'Desdemona')
E–3–Ostrich fern (Matteuccia struthiopteris)
F–10–Golden grass (Hakonechloa macra
  'Aureola')
G–13–Hosta (Hosta gracillima 'variegata')
H–4–Ajuga (Ajuga reptans)
I–1– 'Piedmont Gold' hosta
J–4–Spotted dead nettle (Lamium maculatum
  'White Nancy')
K–1–Pickerel weed (Pontederia cordata)

ALTERNATIVE SELECTIONS

A–3–Heavenly bamboo (Nandina domestica)
B–5–Leather bergenia (Bergenia crassifolia)
D–2–Ligularia (Ligularia tussilaginea)
E–2–Elephant's ear (Colocasia esculenta)
F–10–Variegated sweet flag (Acorus
  gramineus 'Variegatus')
G–13–Mondo grass (Ophiopogon japonicus)
I–1–Kaffir lily (Clivia miniata)

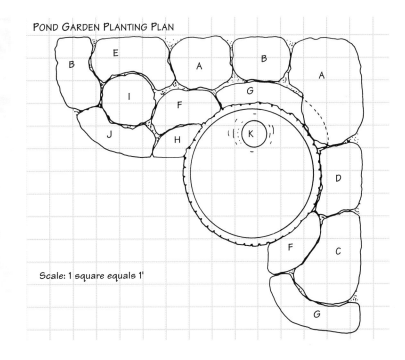

POND GARDEN PLANTING PLAN

Scale: 1 square equals 1'

Near the water's edge, moisture-loving plants such as this emerging Solomon's seal will grow bigger and better each year. This hardy native is also available in a variegated form that sports white and green leaves.

A well-balanced water garden contains three types of aquatic plants: oxygenators, which are submerged plants; floaters that ride on the surface of the water; and bog plants, which grow in shallow water at the pond's edge. You could also include blooming plants such as the water lily in this garden to provide a finishing touch.

A HILLSIDE GARDEN

Once an eyesore, this slope was tamed with a rock wall, waterfall, and extensive plantings.

When a garden changes levels, there is always the problem of the slope. Do you settle for a mediocre lawn, go to the expense of terracing, or choose the monotonous verdure of juniper or ivy? Fortunately, a number of good-looking garden plants are well-suited to life on a hillside. This plan assembles some of the best into a bed that will make the topographical transition worth looking at.

Water penetrates poorly on sloping ground; some of it runs off before it soaks in. And sloping land often is composed of shallow or poor soil, especially if the slope is a land cut. Consequently, a good hillside plant has to be a tough one, able to thrive in marginal soils with something less than routine garden watering. All of these plants are equal to that challenge. However, to give them a chance to look their best, you should dig the soil well before planting, then water regularly until the planting is established. Be sure this hillside bed will receive full sun.

The main planting list is for Zones 6 through 9; in Zones 6 and 7, the variegated common sage may perish in exceptionally cold winters, but spring replacement plants will fill in quickly. The alternative selections should be used in dry-summer Zone 10 and may be chosen for gardens in dry-summer Zone 9.

The flowering quince kicks off the color display in late winter or early spring when its bare branches deck themselves in pink or red flowers. After it has finished blooming, it becomes a twiggy, leafy backdrop to its summer-flowering neighbors. The main planting scheme is at its most colorful from early to late summer, beginning with the 'Vancouver Gold' broom. Among the alternative selections, the feathery cassia flowers in late winter and early spring, the rock rose and two morning glories bloom in spring, and the Mexican bush sage puts on a lavish purple display in late summer and fall.

HILLSIDE GARDEN PLANTING PLAN

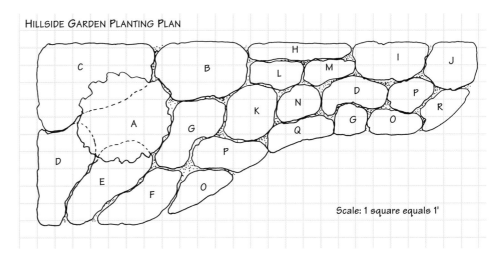

Scale: 1 square equals 1'

To maintain this garden, go over it in late winter or early spring with shears in hand. Remove all the dead stems of the perennials, which bore last year's flowers. Cut back the Russian sage and bluebeard to about 6 inches. Cut back halfway the English lavender, southernwood, common wormwood, variegated common sage, and catmint. To keep the plants compact, shear back the broom, lavender cotton, and wall germander as needed. If the dead leaves won't be unsightly, you might want to leave them in place as a mulch. Mulches aid water penetration, retard evaporation, and moderate soil temperature—three characteristics that particularly benefit plants growing on a hillside. After several years, you may need to dig up and divide the two kinds of yarrow and coreopsis if the plantings are crowded.

VARIATIONS

If the maximum planting depth of 10 feet is greater than you need, you can reduce it to 7 feet. Eliminate the English lavender (D), lavender cotton (E), lanceleaf coreopsis (F), and catmint (O). Add one more plant of broom (C) to finish off the new edge.

HILLSIDE GARDEN PLANTS

A–1–Flowering quince (Chaenomeles)
B–2–Russian sage (Perovskia atriplicifolia)
C–3–Broom (Genista pilosa 'Vancouver Gold')
D–7–English lavender (Lavandula angustifolia)
E–5–Lavender cotton (Santolina chamaecyparissus)
F–5–Lanceleaf coreopsis (Coreopsis lanceolata)
G–7–Daylily (Hemerocallis, dark yellow cultivar)
H–5–Daylily (Hemerocallis, red cultivar)
I–2–Bluebeard (Caryopteris × clandonensis)
J–1–Southernwood (Artemisia abrotanum)
K–1–Common wormwood (Artemisia absinthium)
L–3–Fern-leaf yarrow (Achillea filipendulina 'Coronation Gold')
M–2–Variegated garden sage (Salvia officinalis 'Icterina')
N–2–Japanese blood grass (Imperata cylindrica 'Rubra')
O–4–Catmint (Nepeta × faassenii)
P–5–Yarrow (Achillea 'Moonshine')
Q–3–Wall germander (Teucrium chamaedrys)
R–2–Threadleaf coreopsis (Coreopsis verticillata 'Zagreb')

ALTERNATIVE SELECTIONS
A–1–Feathery cassia (Senna artemisioides)
B–2–Mexican bush sage (Salvia leucantha)
C–3–Sageleaf rock rose (Cistus salviifolius)
H–4–African lily (Agapanthus orientalis)
I–2–Bush morning glory (Convolvulus cneorum)
Q–3–Ground morning glory (Convolvulus sabatius)

Any low-growing perennial or herb is ideal for growing in a stone wall. Dianthus, for example, is compact by nature and won't require more wall space when it matures. It also thrives on the quick drainage provided by the wall.

GARDENS FOR
SPECIFIC PLANTS

Half the fun of gardening is mixing and matching flowers, shrubs, herbs, and vegetables in the same garden. But sometimes creating a garden that contains similar plants makes the most sense. Flowering shrubs, for example, generally require more space than most other plants, so are better off planted in a bed or border all their own. Garden design can also play a part in your decision to have a specific plants garden. Formal rose gardens are a good example. They're designed to display roses in rigid geometric beds where free-flowing annuals and perennials would look out of place. In this chapter, you'll discover some stunning gardens, all of which are built on a single family of blooming plants.

Gardens devoted to one type of plant can add impact and drama to your landscape. Roses in particular are especially beautiful when planted together like these pink and red Shrub roses. They're a garden in themselves.

AN ANNUALS GARDEN

As versatile as they are colorful, petunias are reliable summer bloomers. They are available in miniature, standard, and spreading varieties.

Use annuals to transform open spaces in any garden into bold displays of beauty. In this annual border, blue salvia, nasturtium, begonia, and marigold create a rainbow of color.

Evaluated in flowers per square foot, no other planting quite matches the output of a bed of annuals. Give these plants the same type of care you would give a vegetable garden, and you'll have nonstop color throughout most of the growing season. Their rapid growth to flowering size nearly puts them into the "instant landscape" category, a point especially appreciated by the new homeowner facing a bare expanse of soil and by any gardener with limited space. Another virtue of annuals is their great adaptability. Many of the popular kinds thrive in diverse climates. The petunias that you see on Cape Cod are the same kind you might find in Omaha or Phoenix.

This garden focuses on warm-season or summer annuals that give the longest-running performance. The flowers will thrive in all parts of Zones 3 through 10 except the humid-summer part of Zone 10 and high-latitude regions where summers are both cool and short. The main plant list features bright colors, including orange and gold shades; the alternative selections replace strident colors with softer tones plus

pink, rose, and magenta. Select a garden spot in full sun, then prepare the soil as you would for a vegetable plot, digging in organic amendments and fertilizer. Set out young plants when there is no longer any danger of frost preferably after the soil has warmed.

During the growing season, your maintenance work should be aimed at keeping the plants growing actively. Water as often as needed during spring and summer. Just as with vegetables, productivity is enhanced by maintaining steady growth unhindered by periods of drought. It's also a good idea to remove spent flowers periodically. This keeps the plants from diverting their energies from flower production to seed setting. When colder weather or frost spells an end to the flowering season, you may remove the plants or leave them in place over winter. In colder

ANNUALS GARDEN PLANTS

A–3–Mexican sunflower (*Tithonia rotundifolia*)
B–1–Four-o-clock (*Mirabilis jalapa*)
C–6–African marigold (*Tagetes erecta*, yellow selection)
D–7–Yellow cosmos (*Cosmos sulphureus*, 'Klondike')
E–7–Zinnia (*Zinnia elegans*, red, orange, or yellow selection)
F–8–African marigold (*Tagetes erecta*, orange selection)
G–5–Scarlet sage (*Salvia splendens*, purple selection)
H–6–Calliopsis (*Coreopsis tinctoria*)
I–9–Dahlia, bedding, bronze-leaved selection
J–4–Snow-on-the-mountain (*Euphorbia marginata*)
K–12–Pot marigold (*Calendula officinalis*, cream selection)
L–8–Cockscomb (*Celosia argentea cristata* 'Plumosa', gold selection)
M–10–Ageratum (*Ageratum houstonianum*)
N–7–Flowering tobacco (*Nicotiana alata* 'Lime Green')
O–14–Sweet alyssum (*Lobularia maritima*)
P–5–Creeping zinnia (*Sanvitalia procumbens*)
Q–6–Petunia (*Petunia x hybrida*, blue selection)
R–4–Blanket flower (*Gaillardia pulchella*)

S–5–Bells of Ireland (*Moluccella laevis*)
T–5–Scarlet sage (*Salvia splendens*, lavender selection)
U–8–Mexican zinnia (*Zinnia haageana*)
V–4–Petunia (*Petunia x hybrida*, yellow selection)

ALTERNATIVE SELECTIONS

A–4–Spider flower (*Cleome* 'Helen Campbell')
B–6–Annual mallow (*Lavatera trimestris*)
C–6–African marigold (*Tagetes erecta*, light yellow selection)
D–7–Cosmos (*Cosmos bipinnatus* 'Candystripe')
E–7–Zinnia (*Zinnia elegans*, magenta selection)
F–8–African marigold (*Tagetes erecta*, yellow selection)
H–6–Pincushion flower (*Scabiosa atropurpurea*)
I–9–Dahlia, bedding type, cream or yellow selection
N–7–Flowering tobacco (*Nicotiana* 'Nicki Hybrids')
P–13–Annual phlox (*Phlox drummondii*)
R–4–Vinca (*Catharanthus roseus*, white)
U–7–Sea lavender (*Limonium latifolium*)

regions—especially where snow falls—you might leave them in place because the untidy appearance of the garden in winter will be less of an issue and birds may appreciate seeds that form from the last set of flowers. In late winter or early spring, when the soil is workable, dig or till the bed, replenish organic amendments and fertilizers, and prepare for another planting season.

VARIATIONS

This planting, which is 8 feet from front to back, was designed as an island bed accessible from all sides. If you want a shallower bed to plant against a wall or fence, you can draw a line between the dots at either end of the plan, and omit all the plants in the smaller segment. This will give you a bed

of the same length but only 6 feet deep. If you choose this option, plant just nine pot marigolds (K), four yellow (or the alternative light yellow) African marigolds (C), and two ageratum (M).

ANNUALS GARDEN PLANTING PLAN

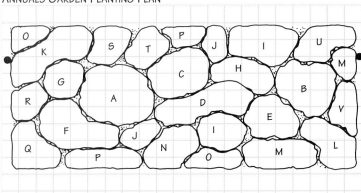

Scale: 1 square equals 1'

A PERENNIALS GARDEN

A mix of perennials creates a tapestry of color and form in your garden. This bed includes hosta, cranesbill, perennial sage, bearded iris, and lady's mantle.

Every year, a garden of perennials comes back like a reunion of faithful old friends. They reappear at their appointed times, mingle graciously, then depart one by one—leaving you with the cleanup. An annual tidying is a small price to pay for the bountiful flowers that perennials produce year after year. You can leave most perennials in place for many years before they will need replanting to restore their energies; others are permanent.

This garden of perennials contains some all-time favorites as well as a few less widely known kinds whose virtues should be better appreciated. The display will be summer-long, starting in late spring with Siberian iris and concluding in fall with Frikart's aster, stonecrop, sundrops, and perhaps a second flowering of beard-tongue and daylilies. Dominating the scene are the colewort, with airy 8-foot flower panicles, and the shrubby false indigo. Around them are plants that offer a great variety of leaf shapes, sizes, and textures, and flowers in colors from cool to warm, pale to bright. Good, well-drained soil, sun for most of the day, and routine watering will satisfy this set of plants. The main plant list contains perennials that will succeed in Zones 5 through 9, given routine watering. Gardeners in dry-summer Zone 10 should plant the alternative selections; gardeners in dry-summer Zone 9 may choose either list.

Prepare the planting area as though you were going to set out annuals or vegetables. Because perennials frow in place for at least three years, they greatly benefit from thorough soil preparation. They'll need a yearly cleanup of dead foliage and spent flowering stems. In warmer zones, complete the cleanup in late fall or winter; where freezing winters are the rule, you can delay the work until early spring, but fall is preferable. A few of the perennials will need further trimming. Where catmint foliage remains alive over winter, cut back the stems by about half before spring growth starts to

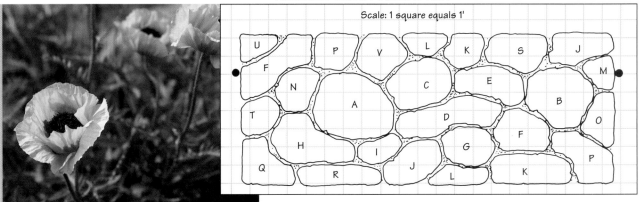

PERENNIALS GARDEN PLANTING PLAN

Scale: 1 square equals 1'

Oriental poppies are a welcome sight in the June perennial border. They require a sunny spot and well-drained soil.

keep the plants compact. Among the alternative selections, cut back the artemisia by half, and lightly head back the ground morning glory and Mexican daisy as needed to keep the plants from becoming rangy. Apply an all-purpose fertilizer just as growth begins each year.

How often you need to dig up and divide perennials depends on the particular perennial, the culture it receives, and your climate (plants in the warmer zones often need more frequent dividing). Crowded clumps and declining performance are your best indicators that dividing is needed. If you use the main list, in two or three years you may need to replace the mallow and beard-tongue. Every three or four years, you may need to divide and replant the yarrows, Shasta daisy, sage, threadleaf coreopsis, coral bells, Frikart's aster, stonecrop, and sundrops. The daylilies and Siberian iris can go longer. The catmint and cranesbill are less predictable; divide and replant them, or start new plants, whenever their performance declines. Consider these as permanent plants: colewort, false indigo, baby's breath, balloon flower, and lady's mantle.

If you use the alternative selections, you may need to replace the artemisia and toadflax every four or five years (you can start new plants from cuttings). Dig, divide, and replant the dahlia about every three years—also the vervain, to keep it from overrunning its neighbors. Divide or replace the ground morning glory and Mexican daisy only when reduced vigor indicates the need. The gaura and lily-of-the-Nile can remain undisturbed.

VARIATIONS

This bed was designed to be viewed from all sides. For a narrower planting to go along a wall or fence, you can easily cut the depth

PERENNIALS GARDEN PLANTS

A–1–Colewort (*Crambe cordifolia*)
B–1–False indigo (*Baptisia australis*)
C–1–Baby's breath (*Gypsophila paniculata* 'Bristol Fairy')
D–5–Fern-leaf yarrow (*Achillea filipendulina* 'Coronation Gold')
E–7–Mallow (*Malva alcea*)
F–12–Shasta daisy (*Leucanthemum* × *superbum*)
G–1–Balloon flower (*Platycodon grandiflorus*)
H–9–Sage (*Salvia superba*)
I–2–Siberian iris (*Iris siberica* 'Ego')
J–4–Cranesbill (*Geranium endressii* 'Wargrave Pink')
K–5–Stonecrop (*Sedum spathulifolium*)
L–5–Daylily (*Hemerocallis* 'Stella de Oro')
M–2–Daylily (*Hemerocallis* 'Bertie Ferris' or other orange-apricot miniature cultivar)
N–2–Daylily (*Hemerocallis*, tall light yellow selection)
O–2–Catmint (*Nepeta* x *faassenii*)
P–3–Threadleaf coreopsis (*Coreopsis verticillata* 'Moonbeam')
Q–3–Lady's mantle (*Alchemilla mollis*)
R–4–Coral bells (*Heuchera sanguinea*)
S–5–Yarrow (*Achillea* 'Moonshine')
T–3–Beard-tongue (*Penstemon barbatus* 'Prairie Fire')
U–1–Sundrops (*Oenothera fruticosa*)
V–2–Frikart's aster (*Aster frikartii*)

ALTERNATIVE SELECTIONS
A–3–Dahlia, bush type, yellow, bronze, or peach selection
C–1–Artemisia (*Artemisia arborescens*)
E–3–Gaura (*Gaura lindheimeri*)
G–2–Vervain (*Verbena rigida*)
I–3–Toadflax (*Linaria maroccana*)
J–4–Mexican daisy (*Erigeron karvinskianus*)
N–2–Lily-of-the-Nile (*Agapanthus orientalis*)
Q–2–Ground morning glory (*Convolvulus mauritanicus*)

from 8 feet to 6 feet. Draw a line connecting the dots on the ends, then omit the plants in the smaller portion. This will eliminate the sundrops (U), Frikart's aster (V), yarrow (S), daylily (M), four Shasta daisies (F) in one plant group, and one plant group each of threadleaf coreopsis (P), 'Stella de Oro' daylily (L), stonecrop (K), and cranesbill (J).

An Ornamental Grasses Garden

No longer are grasses to be viewed as weeds or as plants to be sheared into subjugation as a lawn. Ornamental grasses—long on the periphery of horticulture—have come into the mainstream and are being recognized for their distinct beauty in form, texture, and color. This planting brings together the most commonly available grasses.

Featured in this garden are fountain grass in the foreground and 'Stricta' feather reed grass in the background. Both provide color and interest in the garden throughout the year and are particularly striking when they rustle in the wind over a thick blanket of snow.

Adaptability is characteristic of these grasses. Plants in both lists grow in Zones 5 through 9 and dry-summer Zone 10. The main list contains grasses that will prosper in a sunny bed; substituting the three alternative selections (including a grasslike sedge) gives you a planting you can use in light shade. Best performance, in either case, will derive from well-drained soil and routine watering.

You'll find that this bed of ornamental grasses makes relatively few maintenance demands. Aside from watering during dry periods, an annual cleanup of dead leaves and stems is the only routine to put on your

schedule. All but three of the grasses (blue oat grass, blue fescue, and tufted hair grass) and the sedge are deciduous, growing an entirely new set of leaves each spring. Cleaning up deciduous grasses is simple: Cut dead material nearly to the ground. With the evergreen kinds, pull out dead leaves from the clumps (though you can give the blue fescue a close trim when it looks unkempt). The timing for the annual cleanup depends on your climate and personal preference. The dead foliage and flower stalks may remain attractive, weather permitting, well into winter, so that you could delay cleanup, if you wished, until just before the start of new growth. In warmer areas, cut back dead leaves and stems any time from late fall to late winter or early spring. In snowy regions, leave the foliage and stems through the winter. Most ornamental grasses will thrive for years without dividing and replanting. The exception in this plan is the blue fescue: When clumps decline in vigor, dig them up and replant small divisions.

Although this planting was designed to wrap around a corner, you can make a simple corner planting by cutting

Although ornamental grasses look good in a garden all their own, they also work well as accent plants in mixed perennial borders. Plant tall varieties in the back of the garden; surround them with complementary annuals and perennials. Shorter grasses make fine edging plants.

Ornamental grasses are at their best in fall and winter when their seed stalks are at their peak. Leave them in place during the winter.

off the wrap. Draw a line from the corner fence post to the dot on the edge of the bed, then omit the plants in the smaller portion. Delete the purple moor grass (C), sea oats (I), three feather reed grass plants (B), and one drift of the Japanese blood grass (D) and blue fescue (H).

ORNAMENTAL GRASSES GARDEN PLANTS

A–1–Maiden grass (Miscanthus sinensis 'Gracillimus')
B–10–Feather reed grass (Calamagrostis acutiflora 'Stricta')
C–3–Variegated purple moor grass (Molinia caerulea 'Variegata')
D–9–Japanese blood grass (Imperata cylindrica 'Rubra')
E–7–Fountain grass (Pennisetum alopecuroides)
F–5–Blue oat grass (Helictotrichon sempervirens)
G–4–Tufted hair grass (Deschampsia caespitosa)
H–12–Blue fescue (Festuca glauca)
I–2–Northern sea oats (Chasmanthium latifolium)
J–1–Colorado blue spruce (Picea pungens 'Glauca')

ALTERNATIVE SELECTIONS
B–6–Maiden grass (Miscanthus sinensis purpurascens 'Autumn Red')
E–7–Tufted sedge (Carex elata)
F–4–Golden grass (Hakonechloa macra 'Aureola')

ORNAMENTAL GRASSES GARDEN PLANTING PLAN

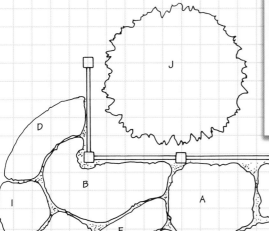

Scale: 1 square equals 1'

A SHRUB BORDER

Few flowering shrubs offer as much color as azaleas. These reliable shrubs develop bowers of bloom every spring. Plant under tall trees or in foundation plantings.

One of the best ways to display flowering shrubs is to pair them with trees that bloom at the same time, like these brightly colored azaleas blooming under a white dogwood canopy.

Although mention of the word shrub may set few gardeners' pulses racing, the vast group of plants covered by that one word includes some of the most attractive and useful garden ornaments. Shrubs are also among the best garden investments. If you choose them carefully, so that they fit their sites, they may last the lifetime of your garden. This border shows that a selection of shrubs chosen for not only their flowers but also foliage colors, textures, and plant shapes can produce a pleasingly varied garden scheme.

There are three plant lists for this border. The main plant list serves gardens in Zones 6 through 9 and is suitable for a sunny location with average, well-drained soil and routine watering. The dominant plants are the purple-leaf sand cherry and the variegated weigela, which has cream and green leaves. Both are deciduous plants, like all the other plants in this list except the wall germander. Foliage color is also provided by the bronze-tinted to yellow spirea and the cranberry cotoneaster and American cranberrybush,

SHRUB BORDER PLANTS

A–1–Purple-leaf sand cherry (Prunus x cistena)
B–1–Variegated weigela (Weigela florida 'Variegata')
C–2–Goldflame spirea (Spiraea japonica 'Goldflame')
D–1–Deutzia (Deutzia x rosea)
E–1–American cranberrybush (Viburnum trilobum 'Compactum')
F–1–Cinquefoil (Potentilla 'Longacre')
G–3–Wall germander (Teucrium chamaedrys)
H–2–Cranberry cotoneaster (Cotoneaster apiculatus)
I–1–'White Meidiland' rose

ALTERNATIVE SELECTIONS I

A–1–New Zealand tea-tree (Leptospermum scoparium 'Ruby Glow')
B–1–Indian hawthorn (Rhaphiolepis indica 'Pink Cloud')
C–2–Dusty miller (Senecio cineraria)
D–1–Round-leaf mintbush (Prostanthera rotundifolia)

E–1–Pink breath-of-heaven (Coleonema pulchrum)
F–1–Bush morning glory (Convolvulus cneorum)
G–2–Dwarf pomegranate (Punica granatum 'Chico')
H–2–Trailing rosemary (Rosmarinus officinalis 'Prostratus')
I–2–Australian fuchsia (Correa pulchella)

ALTERNATIVE SELECTIONS II

A–1–Japanese camellia (Camellia japonica 'Mrs. D.W. Davis')
B–1–Bigleaf hydrangea (Hydrangea macrophylla 'Tricolor')
C–2–Azalea (Rhododendron 'Ward's Ruby')
D–1–Camellia (Camellia hiemalis 'Shishi-Gashira')
E–1–Azalea (Rhododendron 'Sherwood Orchid')
F–1–Azalea (Rhododendron 'Albert Close' and 'Elizabeth')
G–2–David viburnum (Viburnum davidii)
H–1–Azalea (Rhododendron 'Fielder's White')
I–2–Azalea (Rhododendron 'Gumpo Pink')

which offer vivid red fall foliage. The flowering season starts in early spring with a cloud of pink blossoms on the purple-leaf sand cherry; a little later in spring there's a burst of pink flowers on the deutzia and white flowers on the cranberry cotoneaster. The 'White Meidiland' rose starts to flower in spring and continues blooming through fall. In late spring to summer, blooms appear on the weigela (dark rose), American cranberrybush (white), cinquefoil (yellow), spirea (rosy red), and wall germander (lilac). In fall, the bright red fruits on the American cranberrybush and cranberry cotoneaster produce a final show.

The Alternative Selections I plant list is a mostly evergreen assortment of plants suitable for dry-summer Zones 9 and 10. They do best in a bed with average, well-drained soil in a sunny location and regular watering. The most prominent plant is the New Zealand tea-tree, which is covered with glowing crimson flowers in late winter and spring. Also flowering at this time are the trailing rosemary, spangled with small blue blossoms; the Australian fuchsia, which produces bell-shaped, deep red flowers; the pink breath-of-heaven, a froth of tiny flowers and leaves; and the Indian hawthorn, which usually starts its

SHRUB BORDER PLANTING PLAN

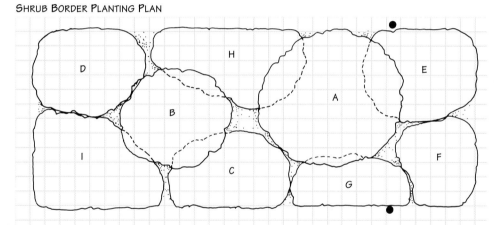

Scale: 1 square equals 1'

clusters of pink flowers in winter. This alternative list also offers foliage variety: The dusty miller and bush morning glory are silvery gray; the Australian fuchsia, gray-green; the pomegranate, glossy bright green with yellow fall color.

Alternative Selections II makes a border of winter- and spring-flowering azaleas and camellias, an excellent choice for Zones 8 and 9 in the South and Southeast and Zones 8, 9, and 10 on the Pacific coast.

VARIATIONS

To shrink this shrub border, draw a line between the two dots and eliminate the two plants in the smaller portion: American cranberrybush (E) and cinquefoil (F).

A FORMAL MODERN-ROSE GARDEN

Roses are a universally beloved flower, grown in both hemispheres and on all continents but Antarctica. From early in the 19th century, plant breeders have been working creatively with roses, producing the rainbow array of blossoms that we take for granted.

As it evolved in Europe, the traditional rose garden was frequently formal, often a series of rectangular units. Here is just such a formal layout, featuring the most popular classes of Modern roses. The main plant list includes a sampling of the range of colors in Modern roses but with a pink-red emphasis. The alternative selections feature warm yellow-orange tones.

One reason for the global popularity of roses is that, given the necessary protection from frosts and pests and diseases, roses will grow in a broad range of climates. Conceivably, you could plant this garden in any of the USDA zones, although in the coldest zones you would need to protect the plants and perhaps replace a few each spring. The common boxwood has a more limited climate tolerance than the roses, thriving in moist- or cool-summer Zones 6 through 10, although a few cultivars, such as the 'Welleri' and 'Vardar Valley', will grow in Zone 5 as well. In Zones 3, 4, and 5, substitute the inkberry holly from the alternative selections list. In dry-summer Zones 7 through 10, you can use the Japanese boxwood alternative selection.

Roses appreciate good soil, sun for at least 6 hours a day, and regular watering. For all the rewards roses give you, the extra maintenance they may need is well-earned. Late winter (in Zones 8, 9, and 10) or early to mid-spring (in colder zones) is pruning time. Just as the new growth starts to

FORMAL MODERN-ROSE GARDEN PLANTING PLAN

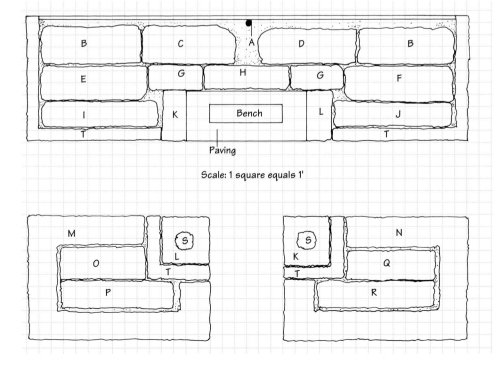

Scale: 1 square equals 1'

Hybrid Tea, Floribunda, and Grandiflora roses give you an almost unlimited color palette to work with. Once established, these spectacular plants are in almost constant bloom. Cut flowers frequently to encourage more bloom.

break, cut out any dead or weak stems and head back the other stems to keep the plant healthy and encourage strong new growth that will bear the flowers. After pruning, many rose growers apply a dormant spray to kill any overwintering fungus spores or eggs of various pests. During the growing season, water the bushes regularly to keep them healthy and productive; apply fertilizers, and spray for pests and diseases as needed. Throughout spring and summer, remove spent blossoms.

In Zones 3 through 6, where freezing winter temperatures are likely to kill any exposed plants, you need to protect your roses in late fall to ensure their survival. Some Zone 7 growers also find minimal protection helpful.

There are a number of ways to protect rosebushes. For example, you can mound soil around them, you can enclose them in protective cones or cylinders, or you can completely bury them. For additional information on winter protection and other aspects of rose care, refer to Ortho's *All About Roses.*

VARIATIONS

This formal design comprises three separate beds that together form a unified rose garden. However, the large single bed can stand alone as an individual planting where only a narrow space is available.

When creating a formal rose garden, avoid the temptation to plant one specimen of every rose variety. Instead, plant groupings of the same variety for a more harmonious color show.

FORMAL MODERN-ROSE GARDEN PLANTS

A–1–'Handel' (large-flowered Climber)
B–4–'Queen Elizabeth' (Grandiflora)
C–2–'Mister Lincoln' (Hybrid Tea)
D–2–'Pascali' (Hybrid Tea)
E–3–'Double Delight' (Hybrid Tea)
F–3–'Miss All-American Beauty' (Hybrid Tea)
G–4–'French Lace' (Floribunda)
H–3–'Cherish' (Floribunda)
I–4–'Class Act' (Floribunda)
J–4–'Angel Face' (Floribunda)
K–16–'Over the Rainbow' (Miniature)
L–16–'Cupcake' (Miniature)
M–13–'Europeana' (Floribunda)
N–13–'Amber Queen' (Floribunda)
O–2–'Sheer Bliss' (Hybrid Tea)
P–3–'Perfume Delight' (Hybrid Tea)

Q–2–'Fragrant Cloud' (Hybrid Tea)
R–3–'Granada' (Hybrid Tea)
S–2–'Beauty Secret', standard, in container (Miniature)
T–58–Common boxwood (Buxus sempervirens)

ALTERNATIVE SELECTIONS
A–1–'America' (large-flowered Climber)
B–4–'Gold Medal' (Grandiflora)
C–2–'Duet' (Hybrid Tea)
D–2–'Dolly Parton' (Hybrid Tea)
E–2–'Peace' (Hybrid Tea)
F–3–'Chicago Peace' (Hybrid Tea)
G–4–'Charisma' (Floribunda)
H–3–'Gingersnap' (Floribunda)
I–4–'First Edition' (Floribunda)

J–4–'Summer Fashion' (Floribunda)
K–16–'Yellow Doll' (Miniature)
L–16–'Sheri Anne' (Miniature)
M–13–'Sun Flare' (Floribunda)
N–13–'Showbiz' (Floribunda)
O–2–'Prominent' (Grandiflora)
P–3–'Brandy' (Hybrid Tea)
Q–2–'Sonia' (Grandiflora)
R–3–'Garden Party' (Hybrid Tea)
S–2–'Rainbow's End', standard, in container (Miniature)
T–58–Japanese boxwood (Buxus microphylla japonica) for dry-summer Zones 7 through 10 or for Zones 3 through 5, (40) Inkberry holly (Ilex glabra 'Compacta').

AN INFORMAL MODERN-ROSE GARDEN

Although it is easy to lay out rectangular rose beds—lining up the plants in blocks like parade marchers—introducing curved lines into your plan is the best way to achieve flowing sweeps of color. The broad S curve of this rose garden lends itself to drifts of color, and it will fit easily into a backyard corner.

This plan comprises just 11 rose cultivars, yet they will give you garden color and cut flowers from early spring until frost. The main plant list emphasizes bright, vibrant colors: yellow, orange, bright red, and bronze shades. For a change of pace, look to the alternative selections, which concentrate on a more serene palette of white, lavender, pink, and rich red.

With winter protection, this planting can be grown in Zones 3 through 10. Plant the roses in good garden soil where they will be in sunlight for three-fourths of the day or more.

A regular moisture supply is essential for keeping roses growing well throughout the flowering season. Whenever rainfall isn't abundant—an inch or more each week— watering the roses will be your most routine

For a colorful, low-maintenance plant that works well in any landscape, you can't beat Modern Shrub roses. These tough-as-nails plants are a snap to keep in top form. They grow bigger and better each year.

maintenance task. For other items on this garden's maintenance agenda—including pruning, pest and disease control, and winter protection—refer to the maintenance information in A Formal Modern-Rose Garden on pages 98 and 99.

VARIATIONS

If you lack sufficient space for the full S curve, you can straighten out the front edge of the bed by drawing a line between the dots on the right and left margins. Delete the smaller portion, eliminating the 'Beauty Secret' (K), 'Double Delight' (F), and one of the 'Class Act' (I) roses. Plant the remaining three 'Class Act' roses in a straight line within the allotted space at the front of the bed.

INFORMAL MODERN-ROSE GARDEN PLANTS

A–1–'Joseph's Coat' (large-flowered Climber)
B–3–'Peace' (Hybrid Tea)
C–3–'Ole' (Grandiflora)
D–3–'Mister Lincoln' (Hybrid Tea)
E–1–'Oregold' (Hybrid Tea)
F–3–'Double Delight' (Hybrid Tea)
G–3–'Amber Queen' (Floribunda)
H–4–'Showbiz' (Floribunda)
I–4–'Class Act' (Floribunda)
J–12–'Rainbow's End' (Miniature)
K–9–'Beauty Secret' (Miniature)

ALTERNATIVE SELECTIONS
A–1–'Handel' (large-flowered Climber)
B–3–'Lady X' (Hybrid Tea)
C–3–'White Lightnin' (Grandiflora)
E–1–'Pristine' (Hybrid Tea)
F–3–'Sonia' (Grandiflora)
G–3–'Cherish' (Floribunda)
H–4–'Europeana' (Floribunda)
I–4–'Angel Face' (Floribunda)
J–12–'Peaches 'n' Cream' (Miniature)
K–9–'Toy Clown' (Miniature)

Roses and perennial flowers make ideal partners. In this garden, the single pink flowers of 'Betty Prior' roses and the tall rose-colored spikes of foxglove make an eye-catching combination that will last for weeks in the June border. Other choice partners for Shrub roses include lamb's-ears, catmint, lavender, and pinks.

INFORMAL MODERN-ROSE GARDEN PLANTING PLAN

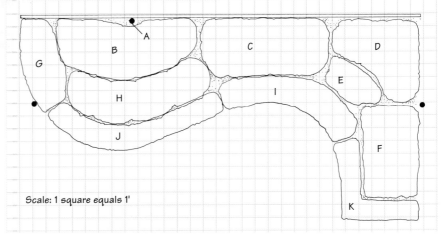

Scale: 1 square equals 1'

AN HEIRLOOM-ROSE GARDEN

By establishing a bed of heirloom roses, you can transport yourself back in time to the gardens of the 19th century. A number of roses that were garden favorites in the 1800s have survived to the present day, cherished and preserved over the generations for their individual beauty and their link to a gracious time gone by. Some of these roses even were known to Napoleon's Empress Josephine, who grew a renowned collection of all the roses known to Western Europe at the time at Malmaison, her palace.

Heirloom-rose enthusiasts recognize two subdivisions among the great array of roses developed before 1900. Old Garden roses are the various classes of roses that derive from European species and were in existence before 1800. These include Gallica, Centifolia, Damask, and Alba roses. With few exceptions, Old Garden roses provide one lavish bloom in mid- to late spring. The introduction of China roses from the Orient, which flower all summer, brought about the development of repeat-flowering classes, including Tea roses, China, Noisette, Bourbon, and Hybrid Perpetuals, and culminated with the Hybrid Teas. The introduction in 1867 of the first Hybrid Tea, 'La France', can be thought of as the dawn of Modern roses, though all roses developed before about 1910 (especially cultivars in the 19th century classes) fall under the "heirloom" umbrella.

This plan creates three different rose gardens. Roses in the main list are Old Garden roses. All give a sumptuous floral display in spring, then rest for the remainder of the year. This group has the broadest adaptability to climate, growing in Zones 4 through 9 and needing no winter protection in the colder zones. In the first list of alternative selections, you'll find 19th century roses that show their China rose ancestry: All flower repeatedly from spring through fall. Less cold-tolerant than the Old Garden roses, these are best in Zones 8, 9, and 10, although gardeners in Zones 5, 6, and 7 may grow some of them—the Bourbon, Hybrid Perpetual, Hybrid Tea, Portland, and Polyantha—if they protect the plants during the winter. The second list of alternatives offers 20th century Shrub roses—technically not heirloom roses, although individually and in mass they give a similar effect. Most are carried by heirloom-rose growers. In cold tolerance, these fall between the roses in the first two lists. Most

Many of the old-fashioned roses available today are rooted in antiquity. Some have played starring roles in gardens for centuries.

will need some winter protection in Zones 4, 5, and 6; the exceptions are 'Carefree Beauty' and 'Frau Dagmar Hartopp'.

The roses on all three lists have the same cultural needs as Modern roses: good soil, sun preferably for at least three-quarters of the day, and regular watering. However, they are in general more forgiving of lapses in culture and turn in good performances with less fuss than their modern relatives. They are also generally more disease-resistant.

VARIATIONS

The paved area with the bench separates this rose planting into two parts of similar shape but unequal size. For a smaller planting, you can eliminate all the roses and companion plants in the smaller portion to the right of the paved area, stopping the planting at the 'Empress Josephine' (I).

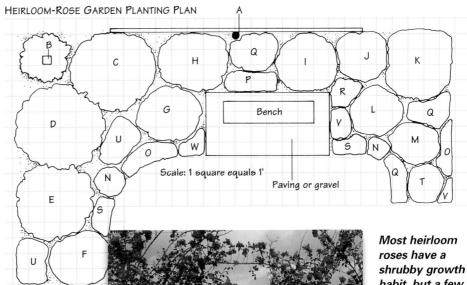

HEIRLOOM-ROSE GARDEN PLANTING PLAN

Scale: 1 square equals 1'

Bench

Paving or gravel

Most heirloom roses have a shrubby growth habit, but a few climbers and ramblers are available. Look for varieties that are hardy in your zone.

HEIRLOOM-ROSE GARDEN PLANTS

A–1–'Complicata' (Gallica hybrid), trained on trellis
B–1–'Mme. Plantier' (Alba hybrid)
C–1–'Communis' ('Common Moss') Moss rose
D–1–'Alba Semi-plena' (Alba hybrid)
E–1–'Marie Louise' (Damask rose)
F–1–'Belle de Crecy' (Gallica rose)
G–1–'Tuscany' (Gallica rose)
H–1–'Mme. Hardy' (Damask rose)
I–1–'Empress Josephine' (Gallica hybrid)
J–1–'Rosa Mundi' (Gallica rose)
K–1–'Celestial' (Alba rose)
L–1–'Rose de Meaux' (Centifolia rose)
M–1–'Burgundian Rose' (Centifolia rose)
N–5–Sweet iris (Iris pallida 'Variegata')
O–7–Catmint (Nepeta x faassenii)
P–2–English lavender (Lavandula angustifolia 'Munstead')
Q–13–Strawberry foxglove (Digitalis x mertonensis)

R–1–Threadleaf coreopsis (Coreopsis verticillata 'Moonbeam')
S–5–Cottage pink (Dianthus plumarius)
T–3–Yarrow (Achillea 'Moonshine')
U–4–Frikart's aster (Aster frikartii)
V–3–Wall germander (Teucrium chamaedrys)
W–4–Coral bells (Heuchera sanguinea)

ALTERNATIVE SELECTIONS I
A–1–'Reve d'Or' (Noisette rose)
B–1–'Sombreuil' (Climbing Tea rose)
C–1–'Gruss an Teplitz' (Bourbon hybrid rose)
D–1–'Duchesse de Brabant' (Tea rose)
E–1–'Archduke Charles' (China rose)
F–1–'Comte de Chambord' (Portland rose)
G–1–'La France' (Hybrid Tea rose)
H–1–'Cecile Brunner' (Polyantha rose)
I–1–'Souvenir de la Malmaison' (Bourbon rose)

J–1–'Reine des Violettes' (Hybrid Perpetual rose)
K–1–'Mme. Lambard' (Tea rose)
L–1–'White Pet' (Polyantha rose)
M–1–'Old Blush' (China rose)

ALTERNATIVE SELECTIONS II
A–1–'Buff Beauty' (Hybrid Musk rose)
B–1–'Cornelia' (Hybrid Musk rose)
C–1–'Betty Prior' (Floribunda rose)
D–1–'Iceberg' (Floribunda rose)
E–1–'Bonica' (Shrub rose)
F–1–'The Yeoman' (Shrub rose)
G–1–'English Garden' (Shrub rose)
H–1–'La Sevillana' (Shrub rose)
I–1–'The Fairy' (Polyantha rose)
J–1–'Carefree Beauty' (Shrub rose)
K–1–'Nevada' (Hybrid Moyesii rose)
L–1–'Frau Dagmar Hartopp' (Hybrid Rugosa rose)
M–1–'Happy' (Polyantha rose)

KEEPING YOUR GARDEN IN TOP FORM

Now that you've had a chance to browse through all 42 garden plans, it's time to get your hands dirty. No matter what style of garden you are interested in, the secrets to success are still the same—good soil, adequate moisture, weed control, fertilizer, and regular maintenance.

Every great garden is built from the ground up. If your soil is mostly sand or clay, you need to do some ground work before you plant. Start by spreading several inches of organic matter over the surface of the soil. Compost, rotted manure, leaf mold, grass clippings, and peat moss are a few of the many organic materials you can use. Then till or spade the entire area to a depth of 6 inches. You may also want to do a soil test to determine whether your soil is acid or alkaline. Acid soils can be improved by adding ground limestone, and alkaline soils can be amended with sulfur. In general, a neutral pH is ideal, although some plants, such as rhododendrons and azaleas, prefer a more acid soil. If you live in rocky or hilly terrain, your best alternative might be to garden in raised beds, where you can easily control soil quality.

After improving the soil, it's time to go plant shopping. When you visit the garden center or nursery, look for stocky, vigorous plants without yellow or dying foliage. Pot size doesn't really matter, because if you're patient, a perennial or annual growing in a 4-inch-wide pot will quickly catch up to—and sometimes surpass—older plants sold in quart- or gallon-sized containers.

If you buy perennials, shrubs, or trees, make sure they'll survive in your region. Just because you find the plant at a local store does not necessarily mean it will tolerate your climate. Read the plant label to find the hardiness zone of the plant. Then use the zone map on page 108 for reference.

The jewel-like blooms of lupines and bearded iris are always a spectacular combination. Both plants require a sunny location with well-drained soil.

GARDENING BASICS

Before you plant a new garden bed, improve the soil by spreading several inches of organic matter over the surface. Then till or spade the organic matter into the top 6 inches of soil. Avoid tilling or spading when the soil is wet.

Wait a few days before planting your new purchases (especially annual, perennial, and vegetable seedlings), which are often fresh from a steamy greenhouse. Put them in a protected location in the garden for a few days so they can become accustomed to the "real world." This process, called hardening off, is an important step to remember, especially in spring.

When your plants are ready to be moved into the garden, avoid transplanting when it's warm and sunny. Cool, overcast weather gives tender transplants a better start, because it inflicts less stress on the plants.

To plant, dig a hole slightly larger than the root ball of the seedling and place the plant in the hole at the same depth it was growing in the nursery pot. Backfill with an improved soil mix and tamp down thoroughly to eliminate air pockets in the soil. Then use a watering can or garden hose to soak the area around the plant. Moisture is vital during the first few days after transplanting. Daily watering is essential if you are growing plants in containers.

After you water, mulch the bed with several inches of shredded bark, cocoa bean hulls, pine needles, or compost. This will eliminate weed competition and help maintain consistent soil moisture.

Research shows that when the air temperature is 100° F a 3-inch layer of mulch can keep the soil underneath up to 25° F cooler. This not only conserves moisture, it also promotes better root growth and more efficient uptake of water and nutrients. When the soil temperature is high, roots stop growing and plants suffer. Newspaper makes an excellent alternative mulch between plants. It keeps roots cool and suppresses weeds. At the end of the season, the newspaper will have partly decomposed and can be easily tilled into the soil. Hide the newspaper under a layer of bark mulch.

A regular, consistent source of moisture is vital to most plants. With the exception of desert locations, most gardens do best with approximately 1 inch of moisture per week. When you water your garden, mark a 1-inch level inside three 1-pound coffee cans and space them around your garden. If less than 1 inch of rain falls during the week following the last watering, use your garden hose or sprinkler to make up the difference. Empty the cans and reset them after each watering or heavy rainfall.

To save time and water, you can install a drip irrigation system. The basic principle is simple: Water is delivered in small quantities under low pressure directly to where it does the most good—the root zones of the plants. This water migrates through the soil by capillary action, so little is lost to evaporation or runoff, especially if you bury the system under a thick layer of mulch. Add a timer, and your watering chores are done automatically, even when you're on vacation.

Plants, especially annuals, roses, and vegetables, need to be fed during the growing season. If you've added compost and/or rotted manure in early spring, you probably don't have to begin feeding your plants until early summer. You can choose from either liquid or dry plant foods. Time-release dry fertilizers can be sprinkled around the base of your plants, where they will provide a slow but steady supply of nutrients over the course of the summer. Liquid fertilizers are a good choice for plants that need a quick boost of energy. You can apply liquid fertilizers in two ways: by mixing them into the water when you irrigate, or by spraying them directly onto the leaves of your plants. This process, called foliar feeding, is probably the fastest way to see results. Many gardeners find that liquid fertilizers work best for annuals, perennials, and vegetables, and time-release dry fertilizers are more useful for lawns, roses, shrubs, and trees.

When you buy a plant food, the ratio of the nutrients will be printed on the label. The numbers indicate the percentage of nitrogen (N), phosphorus (P), and soluble potassium (K), in that order that the fertilizer contains. Thus, a 12-12-12 fertilizer contains 12 percent, by weight, of each nutrient, with the remainder being inert matter.

Nitrogen is necessary for new cell formation in all parts of the plant and is more likely to be lacking in comparison to other nutrients. Because nitrogen is part of both chlorophyll and protein molecules, it's essential to healthy leaf growth.

Phosphorus is required for early growth and development of roots and stems. It also stimulates fruit and seed production. Phosphorus deficiency is most likely the cause when leaves take on a red or purplish discoloration.

Potassium is essential for strong stems and roots and helps intensify flower color. An acute deficiency of potassium will show up in the form of plants with weak stems and a yellowing and browning of leaves at their tips.

Dividing older plants is necessary with certain species of perennials. Peonies, hostas, chrysanthemums, asters, bearded iris, and daylilies are just a few examples of plants that need to be dug and divided every three to five years. Use a sharp spade or spading fork to lift the plant clump and break it into smaller sections or divisions. Replant the divisions, spacing the plants accordingly.

For the best effect, plant flowers in drifts or clumps. To do this, mark off irregularly shaped planting areas in your border and place separate species or colors in each.

Mixing perennial and annual flowers together in the same garden often has delightful results. In this garden, 'Purple Wave' petunias creep through a bed of perennial black-eyed Susans and 'Moonbeam' threadleaf coreopsis. The petunias provide bold contrast.

USDA Plant Hardiness Zone Map

This map of climate zones helps you select plants for your garden that will survive a typical winter in your region. The United States Department of Agriculture (USDA) developed the map, basing the zones on the lowest recorded temperatures across North America. Zone 1 is the coldest area and Zone 11 is the warmest.

Plants are classified by the coldest temperature and zone they can endure. For example, plants hardy to Zone 6 survive where winter temperatures drop to –10° F. Those hardy to Zone 8 die long before it's that cold. These plants may grow in colder regions but must be replaced each year. Plants rated for a range of hardiness zones can usually survive winter in the coldest region as well as tolerate the summer heat of the warmest one.

To find your hardiness zone, note the approximate location of your community on the map, then match the color band marking that area to the key.

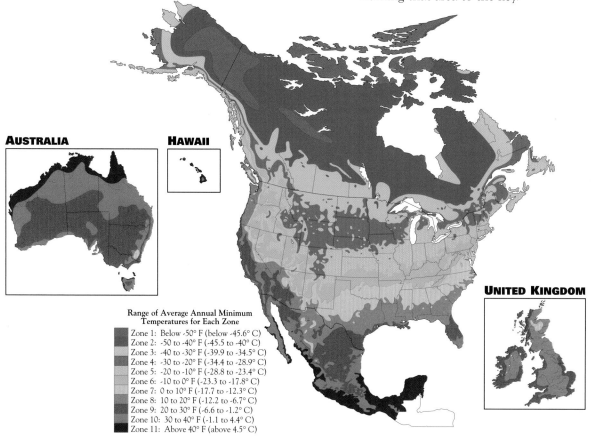

AUSTRALIA

HAWAII

UNITED KINGDOM

Range of Average Annual Minimum Temperatures for Each Zone

Zone 1: Below -50° F (below -45.6° C)
Zone 2: -50 to -40° F (-45.5 to -40° C)
Zone 3: -40 to -30° F (-39.9 to -34.5° C)
Zone 4: -30 to -20° F (-34.4 to -28.9° C)
Zone 5: -20 to -10° F (-28.8 to -23.4° C)
Zone 6: -10 to 0° F (-23.3 to -17.8° C)
Zone 7: 0 to 10° F (-17.7 to -12.3° C)
Zone 8: 10 to 20° F (-12.2 to -6.7° C)
Zone 9: 20 to 30° F (-6.6 to -1.2° C)
Zone 10: 30 to 40° F (-1.1 to 4.4° C)
Zone 11: Above 40° F (above 4.5° C)

METRIC CONVERSIONS

U.S. Units to Metric Equivalents			Metric Units to U.S. Equivalents		
To Convert From	Multiply By	To Get	To Convert From	Multiply By	To Get
Inches	25.4	Millimeters	Millimeters	0.0394	Inches
Inches	2.54	Centimeters	Centimeters	0.3937	Inches
Feet	30.48	Centimeters	Centimeters	0.0328	Feet
Feet	0.3048	Meters	Meters	3.2808	Feet
Yards	0.9144	Meters	Meters	1.0936	Yards

To convert from degrees Fahrenheit (F) to degrees Celsius (C), first subtract 32, then multiply by ⁵⁄₉.

To convert from degrees Celsius to degrees Fahrenheit, multiply by ⁹⁄₅, then add 32.

INDEX
PLANTS IN LANDSCAPE PLANS

Note: Page numbers in *italic type* indicate photographs